Power, Influence, and Persuasion

Harvard Business Essentials

The New Manager's Guide and Mentor

The Harvard Business Essentials series is designed to provide comprehensive advice, personal coaching, background information, and guidance on the most relevant topics in business. Drawing on rich content from Harvard Business School Publishing and other sources, these concise guides are carefully crafted to provide a highly practical resource for readers with all levels of experience, and will prove especially valuable for the new manager. To assure quality and accuracy, each volume is closely reviewed by a specialized content adviser from a world-class business school. Whether you are a new manager seeking to expand your skills or a seasoned professional looking to broaden your knowledge base, these solution-oriented books put reliable answers at your fingertips.

Other books in the series:

Finance for Managers
Hiring and Keeping the Best People
Managing Change and Transition
Negotiation
Business Communication
Managing Projects Large and Small
Manager's Toolkit
Crisis Management
Entrepreneur's Toolkit
Strategy

Power, Influence, and Persuasion

Sell Your Ideas and
Make Things Happen

Harvard Business School Press | *Boston, Massachusetts*

978-1-59139-631-4 (ISBN 13)
Library of Congress Cataloging-in-Publication Data
Harvard business essentials : power, influence, and persuasion.
p. cm.—(Harvard business essentials series)
Includes bibliographical references and index.
ISBN 1-59139-631-X
1. Power (Social sciences)   2. Influence (Psychology)   3. Persuasion
(Psychology)   I. Title: Power, influence, and persuasion.   II. Series.
HM1256.H37 2005
658.4'092—dc22
2004030639

Contents

Introduction

Three executives and their CEO were sitting around a conference table. They were conferring about a matter of importance to them and to most other full-time employees of their four-hundred-person company: How much money would be put into the bonus pool for distribution this year?

Each person at the table had something to say about the matter. The Human Resources vice president understood the details of the bonus system and its impact on employees more than anyone. He argued strenuously for a generous payout, citing the company's strong financial condition and the meager bonus paid the previous year. "People have worked exceptionally hard this year," he said, "and they are expecting to be rewarded in an exceptional way. They've earned it." He went on to describe how the bonus amount he favored fit in with the company's total compensation and benefits package, and he compared that package to those of other employers in the area. The chief operating officer nodded in agreement and offered supporting comments.

The chief financial officer, who had her thumb on current and projected spending activities, was more cautious and argued for a slightly smaller deal. She had substantial influence over the CEO on money matters—so much so that she could trump the wishes of her fellow executives.

These four individuals eventually reached a decision that no other employees were empowered to make. The CEO transmitted that decision to the board of directors for final approval. Only the board could authorize the bonus expenditure. But the board was likely to approve the decision because of the CEO's influence over them. Board members viewed the CEO as credible, effective, and trustworthy. If he said that $1.8 million for the bonus pool was the right number, most board members would accept his judgment, especially if that number was in line with current company performance and future plans. If there were holdouts, the CEO would try to persuade them that his decision was sound. He would cite the endorsements of the vice president of Human Resources, the CFO, and COO—each of whom would be on hand to back up the boss at the board meeting. He would also explain the systematic method used to determine the $1.8 million payout and describe how those bonus funds would motivate employees without jeopardizing pending plans.

This short tale is fabricated, but it reflects how decisions are made in business organizations. And it illustrates the three related ideas explored in this book: power, influence, and persuasion. In this story each of the four executives had influence on the amount of the bonus payout—some more than others. Persuasion was applied where unanimity was absent. The CEO exercised his power in making the bonus payout decision, and the board exercised its power in approving it.

Power, influence, and persuasion have always been part of social systems. One of the more striking examples is found in France's Louis XIV—a seventeenth-century monarch who claimed his power by divine right. Louis considered his power absolute, but he was open to influence by his ministers, seemingly without recognizing it. He leaned heavily on Jean Baptiste Colbert for financial advice, and he looked to the Marquis de Louvois for military strategy. Although Louis made it clear that he would not share authority with any of his ministers, he could not rule without them. Nor could he conceal from them his major personal weakness: an unquenchable fondness for flattery. This weakness provided the channel through which ministers, mistresses, and courtiers applied influence and persuasion. Louvois, for example, used the king's love of praise to steer him into wars he would not otherwise have entered. According to one contemporary, the duke de Saint Simon, Louvois "persuaded him that he had greater talents for war than any of his generals." Thus, even a holder of absolute power is susceptible to influence and persuasion by others, as you will see in this book.

Today's businesses are a far cry from the regime of Louis XIV. Power is no longer absolute but instead is divided among managers, executives, directors, and shareholders. Statutes limit the power of companies and their managers over employees. Formal authority still exists, but the functions served by influence and persuasion have become more important.

What do we mean by these terms? We define *power* as the potential to allocate resources and to make and enforce decisions. For the manager, understanding how to obtain power and use it wisely is an essential, though seldom recognized, skill. John Kotter, a professor of management at Harvard Business School, put it this way:

> *Most managerial jobs require one to be skilled at the acquisition and use of power . . . I suspect that a large number of managers—especially the young, well-educated ones—perform significantly below their potential because they do not understand the dynamics of power and because they have not nurtured and developed the instincts needed to effectively acquire and use power.*[1]

Influence is an extension of power; it is the mechanism through which people use power to change behavior or attitudes. Unlike power, however, influence can produce an effect without the apparent exertion of force, compulsion, or direct command. In a sense, it is power in a velvet glove. (Remember the classic Mafia movie line, "Make him an offer he can't refuse.") In some cases, influence is exerted through manipulation. Influence can also be exercised by people who have no formal power. Every manager must understand how to influence others: bosses, peers, and subordinates.

Persuasion is closely related to influence but is also very different. It isn't a force and has no coercive component. Instead, it is a process through which one aims to change or reinforce the attitudes, opinions, or behaviors of others. Anyone who becomes skilled in the art of persuasion enjoys an edge in selling ideas or products or simply making things happen. Persuasion is an essential life skill, as useful at home as it is in the workplace.

Every business and virtually every human society operates with the help of power, influence, and persuasion. They are as essential to organizational and interpersonal functions as the air we breathe. Every one of us is routinely on the giving or receiving end of power, influence, and persuasion—often simultaneously. Even as we are subject to the power of our bosses, we are influencing and persuading them. And we have similar relationships with our peers and subordinates.

This book will help you to understand these three important concepts, and offers practical advice on how you can put them to work.

L'Éminence Grise

More than a few powerful leaders have been heavily influenced by others. Perhaps one of the most successful and effective of these was Cardinal Richelieu (1585–1642), adviser and ultimately prime minister to Louis XIII. Contemporaries gave him the nickname *éminence rouge* (the red eminence) because of his red clerical garb. A determined advocate of royal power and the bane of anyone who challenged it, Richelieu famously said, "If you give me six lines written by the most honest man, I will find something in them to hang him."

Today many use the term *éminence grise* (the gray, or shadowy, eminence) to refer to anyone who rules from behind the throne or who has unusual power over the formal holder of authority. Éminence grise originally referred to Père Joseph, a French cleric and secretary to Richelieu. Does your organization have its own éminence grise?

What's Ahead

We deal with power, influence, and persuasion in that order. Chapter 1 explains why power is necessary in organizations even though our society distrusts power and those who seek it. It explains three managerial approaches to power and indicates which is best for the organization and the person who wields it.

Where does power come from? Chapter 2 addresses that question. It discusses the characteristics of positional power, relational power, and personal power. It also describes constraints on these powers. For example, the power vested in a position in the organization is naturally limited by the power-holder's dependence on others: peers, bosses, and subordinates. Even with natural constraints, it is possible to increase your power, and you'll learn how in this chapter.

Real power, as described in Chapter 3, is realized only through some form of expression. Influence is one way that power is wielded to change, direct, or affect the behavior of others. This chapter describes the limitations of direct power and explains how managers can use their power indirectly to influence the outcomes they seek. To apply influence, however, people must be open to influence by others; it's a two-way street. This chapter offers a number of practical suggestions for increasing your influence in the organization. Chapter 4 takes the matter of influence a step further by illustrating three specific tactics that any manager can use on the job.

Even for people who have formal power, persuasion is the primary means of changing behavior and affecting decisions. To persuade is to use argument or entreaty to get others to adopt a belief or particular behavior. Chapters 5 and 6 tackle the concept of persuasion. The first of these explains the four elements of persuasion and discusses how various audiences and people with various decision styles are susceptible to different forms of persuasion. Chapter 6 will help you win minds *and* hearts. It explains how to appeal to the logical side of your audience and then goes on to describe techniques for doing the same to their emotional side. It explains how language, vivid descriptions, metaphors, analogies, and stories can help your idea resonate with an audience.

Chapter 7 is about formal presentations, one of the most common opportunities for persuasion in modern business. If you make formal presentations regularly and would like them to be more effective, this chapter can help you. It suggests a presentation structure and a number of rhetorical devices perfected by the ancient Greeks. It also explains the various learning styles used by people and argues why you need to adapt your presentation style to them.

Most of us know the damage that power, influence, and persuasion can cause when handled carelessly, irresponsibly, or with malignant intent. The book's final chapter addresses the ethics problem, suggesting two standards to which power, influence, and persuasion must conform to be considered ethical. And it goes a step further, offering five ways that executives and directors can create an ethical culture within their organization.

When you've finished reading these chapters you'll find several helpful supplementary sections: a glossary of terms, three appendixes, and a list of books and articles you may want to consult as you expand your knowledge of power, influence, and persuasion. The glossary contains terms we've italicized in the chapters. The appendixes contain the following material:

- Appendix A is a short piece titled "Leading When You're Not the Boss." Many people find themselves in situations in which they are expected to lead but have no formal power to do so. Many team leaders, in fact, are outranked by team members. This appendix offers useful tips on how to act in this type of situation.

- Appendix B contains two forms that you may find useful when assessing an audience that you need to persuade and when assessing your own personal ability to persuade others. The first worksheet, "Understanding Your Audience," can also be found online at www.elearning.hbsp.org/businesstools. This worksheet is one of many checklists, worksheets, and interactive tools available to readers without charge (within normal copyright restriction) on the *Harvard Business Essentials* Web site.

- Appendix C explains how to make the most of presentation visuals. Almost everyone uses overheads or projected slides in
  their presentations to management or to their peers and subordinates. Visuals can get key points across and make them memorable. In the wrong hands, however, they can actually confuse
  or bore the audience, diminishing the impact of an entire presentation. This appendix offers commonsense rules for making
  the most of presentation visuals.

1

The Necessity of Power

You Can't Manage Without It

Key Topics Covered in This Chapter

- *Why power and power seekers are suspect*

- *The necessary role of power in organizations*

- *How dependencies restrain the concentration and autocratic use of power*

- *Three managerial approaches to power*

POWER IS A necessary feature of every social system. In military organizations, every unit has one person vested with the power to command action. Even in collegial and democratic workplaces, someone has the authority to say, "Thank you all for your input. Now, here is what must be done." Despite its necessity, however, few people have a positive view of power and are often distrustful of the people who seek it.

This chapter discusses how people feel about power, why it is an essential part of organizational life, and how it is restrained by interpersonal dependencies. It also evaluates three managerial approaches to using power.

Our Antipathy Toward Power

In many cultures, power is viewed with suspicion and fear because of its potential for coercion and corruption. People easily recall examples of power used for malignant purposes rather than for good: Villains such as Hitler, Stalin, Pol Pot, and Saddam Hussein immediately come to mind. The use of power for malicious or self-serving ends is surely what moved Britain's Lord Acton to declare in 1887, "Power tends to corrupt, and absolute power corrupts absolutely." This sentiment is so well entrenched in the public consciousness that those who seek power are viewed with suspicion and distrust. Indeed, many feel that power should be withheld from those who most actively seek it. Because of this general antipathy toward power and power seekers, writes Rosabeth Moss Kanter, "People who have it deny it; people who want it do not want to appear to hunger for it; and people who engage in its machinations do so secretly."[1]

Given our antipathy toward power and those who hold it, it is no surprise that democratic political systems contain checks on power and specify measures to distribute power in ways that prevent it from becoming absolute or concentrated in too few hands. England's Magna Carta (Great Charter), signed in 1215 by King John, provides a concrete example. It stipulated in detail the rights of the church, the barons, and freemen that could not be infringed by the power of the Crown. More than five centuries later, the founders of the American republic grappled with the same issue. Their constitutional solution was to prevent the concentration of power in one branch of government and establish mechanisms that protect the interests of minorities against the power of the majority. The U.S. Constitution's Bill of Rights checks power by specifying individual rights that government cannot abridge.

Power as Necessity

Paradoxically, neither society nor its organizations can function without the application of power. Government cannot fulfill its basic functions without the power to tax and spend, to make laws, and to enforce them. Roadways would be chaotic if police lacked the power to enforce traffic regulations. And our business organizations would quickly go to pieces if boards and managers lacked the power to make and implement strategy, to hire and fire, and to compensate employees. Recognizing the necessity of power, democratic societies allow certain individuals and institutions to have power as long as they use it within the bounds of policy, custom, or law, and in the service of ends that the majority accepts as legitimate.

Power was defined in the Introduction as the potential to allocate resources and to make and enforce decisions. In an organizational context this means that power gives someone the potential, among other things, to do the following:

- Determine compensation for subordinates

- Obtain funding, materials, or staff for key projects

- Have access to important information

- Resolve disputes

- Clear away barriers to progress

- Determine key goals and marshal resources around them

These activities are critical to the business of management; little would be accomplished in the absence of someone's power to decide or act. The power to influence others is equally important. That power can be used to rally support for important goals and to motivate individual employees. It is difficult to think of managers being successful without either type of power.

Paradoxically, societal distrust of individual power does not transfer completely to the workplace, where we expect that some people will have more power than others. In fact, many employees would rather work for managers who have organizational power ("clout") than for people who do not. The former can get them what they want: visibility, upward mobility, and resources. Working for a powerful boss also confers an aura of status on subordinates. In contrast, working for a powerless boss is like being in the outer darkness; subordinates of bosses who have no organizational clout feel powerless and are usually dissatisfied with their situations.

There is even some evidence that powerless bosses are more likely to behave tyrannically toward their underlings. According to Rosabeth Kanter, "Powerlessness . . . tends to breed bossiness rather than true leadership. In large organizations, at least, it is powerlessness that often creates ineffective, desultory management and petty, dictatorial, rules-minded managerial styles."[2] Managers who lack real power cannot obtain the resources needed to fulfill their responsibilities. This leads to frustration, poor morale, and ineffectiveness among subordinates.

Thus, power that is used wisely in workplace settings is more likely to produce effectiveness and motivation than oppression and poor morale. Consider this hypothetical case of a middle manager who, lacking organizational power, has become ineffective:

> *William enjoyed upward mobility during the first six years of his em-*
> *ployment with Ultra Electronix. Hired as a market analyst, he made*
> *important contributions to the company's market research unit, and be-*
> *fore long he was named director of market research. Thanks to his tech-*
> *nical know-how, useful market assessments, and ability to work*
> *productively with other units, William gained progressively more organi-*
> *zational power and influence—and a budget to match. Morale was*
> *high among his five direct reports.*
>
> *William's visibility and growing influence was abetted by his boss,*
> *Harold, the vice president of sales and marketing. Harold believed*
> *strongly in the value of market research and made sure that research*
> *played a key role in high-level product decisions.*
>
> *William's standing in the company changed quickly, however,*
> *when Harold retired. Toni, Harold's successor, had built her career*
> *through the field sales organization and put little stock in formal mar-*
> *ket research. As far as she was concerned, personal relationships with*
> *customers was the be-all and end-all of marketing and market intelli-*
> *gence. So no one was surprised when the budget for market research*
> *was cut 20 percent, forcing William to lay off one of his analysts.*
>
> *Under Toni's regime, William felt his organizational power slipping*
> *away, and with it his ability to influence other managers and motivate*
> *his subordinates. He no longer had exciting projects to offer his people*
> *nor rewards to share. Work became routine and less meaningful. His di-*
> *rect reports no longer looked to him for mentoring or career development.*

Supervisors and managers such as William need power to do their jobs. Lacking it, they exhibit the symptoms described in table 1-1. They develop into managers for whom no one with talent or ambition wants to work. Failing to possess and use power when the situation calls for it results in indecision, delays, and sometimes mischief. As Jeffrey Pfeffer aptly put it in his book *Managing With Power*, "[O]ne can be quite content, quite happy, quite fulfilled as an organizational

TABLE 1-1

Symptoms and Sources of Powerlessness for Key Positions

Position	Symptoms	Sources
First-line supervisors	• Close, rules-minded supervision • Tendency to do things oneself, blocking of subordinates' development and information • Resistant, underproducing subordinates	• Routine, rules-minded jobs with little control over events • Limited lines of information • Few advancement prospects for oneself/ subordinates
Staff professionals	• Turf protection, information control • Retreat into professionalism • Resistance to change	• Routine tasks seen as peripheral to "real" tasks • Blocked careers • Easy replacement by outside experts
Top executives	• Focus on internal cost-cutting, producing short-term results, punishing failure • Dictatorial, top-down communication	• Uncontrollable lines of supply because of environmental changes • Limited or blocked lines of information from below

Source: Adapted from Rosabeth Moss Kanter, "Power Failure in Management Circuits," *Harvard Business Review,* July–August 1979.

hermit, but one's influence is limited and the potential to accomplish great things, which requires independent action, is almost extinguished."[3] People who will not touch the hot handle of power will not—cannot—influence what happens around them.

Of Power and Dependency

If power is essential for effective management, it doesn't necessarily come with the job. Newly minted supervisors and managers usually think that the formal authority attached to their positions will give them all the power they need to fulfill their responsibilities and carve out reputations for themselves in the organization. They believe that, like *Star Trek*'s Captain Picard, they need only describe what they want done and tell subordinates to "make it so." Then reality delivers a swift kick to the posterior. They find that they are not masters of the universe, but highly dependent on others: on their bosses, their subordinates, peers, suppliers, and others.

Dependency is a fact of life in complex organizations, and at every level, because of limited resources and the division of labor and information across many units. Dependency is not eliminated through the acquisition of formal power. Consider these examples:

- Hugh, the manager of a busy coffee and pastry bistro, depends on each crewmember doing his or her job quickly and effectively. Hugh is so busy greeting customers and running the cash register that confusion would reign if there were any laggards.

- William, the director of market research described earlier, depends heavily on the technical know-how of his professional staff to complete his unit's work. Those individuals must design research tools that accurately measure customer demand and preferences. He also depends on people who do not work for him, primarily the company's forty field sales representatives. He needs their intimate knowledge of customers to obtain customer feedback and to identify candidates for focus groups conducted by market research personnel.

- Edgar, the vice president of manufacturing, seldom sees eye-to-eye with the CEO on important issues. In fact, "contained hostility" would be a good description of their relationship. Other executives don't understand why the CEO doesn't fire Edgar and replace him with someone more compliant. The CEO knows the answer: He depends on Edgar's skill in managing the company's production assets. Edgar is hard to work with, but he delivers, and that makes the CEO look good to the board and to shareholders.

- Judith is eager to advance her career. In this she has come to depend on two individuals: her boss, who gives her assignments

that broaden her skills, and Linda, a senior executive with
whom she has established a mentoring relationship. Linda opens
doors for Judith throughout the company and sees that she is assigned to important cross-functional teams.

Each of these examples demonstrates how individuals, even
people with formal authority, depend on others for success.

Although dependency blunts the power that many feel they need in
order to manage, or the power to which they aspire, it serves a crucial purpose in the modern organization. That purpose is to restrain
the concentration and autocratic use of power. Lacking dependencies, leaders and managers would quickly become corrupt and
tyrannical, just as Acton warned. You'll learn more about dependencies in the next chapter.

Using Power: Three Types of Managers

Assuming that people acquire the power they need to do their jobs,
how do they use it, and how does power motivate their behavior?
David McClelland and David Burnham studied these questions and
published their findings in 2003. They found that a manager's approach to power is tightly connected to personal motivation and the
way he or she defines success. In effect, they described three types of
managers: affiliative managers, personal power managers, and institutional managers.[4]

Affliliative Managers

The *affiliative manager,* in the view of McClelland and Burnham, is
more interested in being liked than in having and using power to get
the job done. When dealing with subordinates, this manager's decisions are heavily influenced by what will make subordinates happy
and put them on his side. Consequently, decisions are more ad hoc
than consistent with the requirements of the work at hand. Policies

and procedures are secondary to decisions that make people happy with the boss. Of the three types of managers, this one is the weakest and least effective.

In their eagerness to be liked, affiliative managers fail to use power for its intended purposes. The result is predictable: Key goals are not met. The case of General George B. McClellan (no relation to David McClelland) underscores this important point.

In the early part of the U.S. Civil War (1861–1865), General McClellan was entrusted with the Union's main army, to which he applied his exceptional talents for organizing and training. He built the Army of the Potomac into a powerful fighting machine and developed plans for seizing Richmond, the capital of the secessionist Confederacy. McClellan was popular with his soldiers and with many politicians, who affectionately called him "the Young Napoleon." McClellan basked in that popularity, even to the point of visualizing a political career.

It seems that he was popular with almost everyone except his commander in chief, President Abraham Lincoln. Lincoln repeatedly urged McClellan to use his force to engage the enemy, but the general vacillated. He complained endlessly that he needed more men, more munitions, and more time to prepare. The few campaigns he did launch were either timid, too late, or terminated too quickly. Frustrated by his general's reluctance to use his considerable force, Lincoln sacked him and turned the reins over to others. "My dear McClellan," Lincoln wrote in March 1862, "if you don't want to use the Army I should like to borrow it for a while."

McClellan enjoyed his status and his popularity with the troops and the public, but he didn't use the power he was given to pursue his primary responsibility. So he had to go. Do you know of managers like this—people who are reluctant to make tough decisions and apply their power? The reason for that reluctance, in many cases, is a fear of offending or losing popularity. These managers run the risk of getting a memo similar to the one written by Lincoln: "My dear Jones, if you are fearful of losing the friendship of your subordinates, you will be replaced by someone who has no such fear."

Working for an Affiliative Manager

As much as the affiliative manager will try to be your friend, he will likely jeopardize your career, and for two reasons. First, this manager will not be consistent in making decisions and following policy, and this means that you cannot anticipate his behavior. Second, this manager is likely to lose status in the organization relative to people who know how to acquire power and use it effectively. Consequently you'll be working for a weakened boss and may not get the resources and visibility you need to build your own career. Our advice: Look for a move.

Personal Power Managers

The *personal power manager,* per scholars David McClelland and David Burnham, is a much different creature. This manager's personal need for power exceeds his need to be liked. He seeks power for himself and for people on his team in order to get the job done. Unlike the authoritarian or coercive boss, who gains strength by making everyone around him weak, this boss generally manages in a democratic way. Subordinates like this kind of boss and often become very loyal because their boss is strong and makes them feel strong. On the negative side, these managers are power aggrandizers and turf builders, and not good institution builders. Consider this example:

Steve, the vice president of corporate sales, is smart, aggressive, and a tough taskmaster. During his first year in his current post, he pushed out the three or four people who couldn't or wouldn't do their jobs, replacing them with individuals having solid track records. "You people are on the best team in the business," he often tells his staff and sales representatives.

Steve is generous with his subordinates and stands behind them when they come into conflict with people in other departments. "We are sales," he likes to remind them during periodic pep talks. "Nothing happens in this company until one of us makes a sale. Nothing! That's something that other departments need to understand."

Although Steve has met the company's sales goals and has built high energy and morale in his unit, he has created friction with other departments—to the point that collaboration has become difficult. To Steve, every interaction with other departments is an opportunity either to defend the prerogatives of his unit from encroachment or to expand its power at another department's expense.

Do you know any managers like Steve? If you do, you know that they are not team players in the companywide sense. They are fiercely competitive and often combative in their interactions with fellow managers. And when they eventually exit the company for more powerful positions elsewhere, the subordinates they leave behind feel as though the air has been sucked out of them because their loyalties were to their boss, and not to the larger organization.

Working for the Personal Power Manager

If you work for a personal power manager, expect a high sense of team spirit within your unit. However, the boss may have so estranged other departments that collaboration with people outside your unit will be difficult. You may also find yourself forced to choose between the interests of your unit (i.e., your boss) and the interests of the company as a whole. In the long term this may endanger your career with the company, especially if and when the personal power boss departs. The best advice in these situations is as follows:

- Be loyal to your boss—this boss demands and rewards loyalty—but only as long as you are not required to do anything that is clearly against the interests of the company and its shareholders.

- Build and maintain your own broad network of contacts within the company; doing so will increase your effectiveness.

- Develop a personal reputation for high integrity and standards; that reputation will help you if and when your boss leaves the company.

Institutional Managers

The most effective managers, say McClelland and Burnham, have something in common with personal power types such as Steve (see figure 1-1). They need power more than they need to be liked. But that's where the similarity ends. These *institutional managers* deploy power in the service of the organization, and not in service of personal goals. Generally, these people

- are highly organization-minded

- have a strong work ethic

- are willing to sacrifice some self-interest for the welfare of the organization

- believe in rewarding individuals who work hard toward organizational goals.[5]

For subordinates who like to work hard and do a good job, these are the best managers to work for: They are mature—not egotistical and not defensive—and eager to reward performance.

Altering Your Management Style

Can you change your management style? Yes, according to McClelland and Burnham—but only after you become aware of your current style. You can gain this self-awareness through executive coaching or by seeking objective feedback from peers and subordinates.

Awareness must be followed by behavior change. For example, if you find that you are an affiliative manager and you want to become an institutional manager, you must adopt the behaviors of that type of person and make habits of those behaviors. Perhaps the most fruitful way to accomplish this is to identify and emulate a successful role model—someone who has the traits of an institutional manager. If you can, get yourself assigned to that person as a subordinate. If

FIGURE 1-1

Assessing the Effectiveness of Manager Types

WHICH MANAGER IS MOST EFFECTIVE?

Subordinates of managers with different motive profiles report different levels of responsibility, organizational clarity, and team spirit.

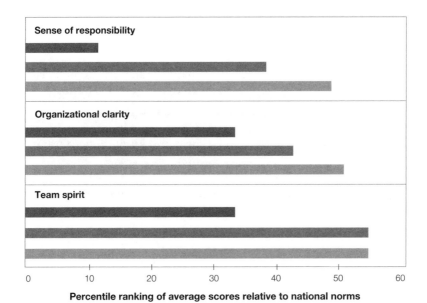

Percentile ranking of average scores relative to national norms

Scores for at least three subordinates of:

- ■ Affiliative managers (affiliation greater than power, high inhibition)
- ■ Personal-power managers (power greater than affiliation, low inhibition)
- ▨ Institutional managers (power greater than affiliation, high inhibition)

Source: David C. McClelland and David H. Burnham, "Power Is the Great Motivator," *Harvard Business Review,* January 2003, 123.

that is not possible, ask that manager to become your mentor. If all else fails, observe the institutional manager from a distance. Take note of how she makes decisions and works with peers, superiors, and subordinates. Then imitate what you observe.

Yes, power is necessary, and individuals embody and use it in various ways. You cannot manage without it. But if it is necessary, what are its sources? That's the subject of the next chapter.

Summing Up

- People generally distrust and fear power and those who seek it.

- Despite negative views of power, organizations cannot function without it. Most people prefer working for bosses who have and use power.

- New managers quickly discover that their power to act is limited by dependencies on others.

- According to two researchers, affiliative managers are ineffective users of power; they are more interested in being liked than in having and using power to accomplish goals.

- Personal power managers seek power and know how to use it. However, their use of power is often self-serving.

- Institutional managers, as described in this chapter, represent the ideal. They use power to advance the interests of the organization, giving those interests priority over their own.

Power Sources

How You Can Tap Them

Key Topics Covered in This Chapter

- *The power of position and its limitations*

- *How dependencies limit positional power*

- *Relationships with others as a source of power*

- *Using coalitions to increase relational power*

- *The law of reciprocity*

- *The sources of personal power*

- *An extended example of personal power*

- *Identifying power sources in your company*

POWER IS A necessary element of organizational work. The question is, What are its sources? Power in organizations generally has three sources:

- **Position.** Your position in the organization confers some level of formal power.

- **Relationships.** Informal power stems from your relationship with others.

- **Personal.** Some people generate power from within; that power is based on general knowledge, technical competence, and an ability to articulate ideas or a vision that others will follow.

This chapter will help you understand these three sources. Once you understand them, you'll find ways to increase your own power—power you can use to achieve goals large and small.

The Power of Position

Power of position derives from your formal position in the organization. That position is usually invested with a title, a set of responsibilities, some level of authority to act, and control of specific resources. Neither a title nor a set of official responsibilities, however, is a true source of power. Real power resides in the authority to act and to control resources that others want or need, including the following:

- Career-enhancing assignments for subordinates
- Permission to form a project and move it forward
- Approval of budgets, work plans, and vacation schedules
- The power to appraise performance
- Money (via control or influence over the budgeting process)
- Promotions and pay raises
- Materials and equipment
- Information

Formal positions in an organization carry with them a certain amount of authority. The CEO, for example, is the ultimate arbiter of decisions, barring vetoes by the board of directors. By virtue of his position, the CEO can determine who is hired and fired, how financial resources will be allocated, and so forth. This *power of position* is also observable at lower levels. An inventory manager will usually have the final say on stock levels and reorder sizes. Although her boss has the power to overrule her decisions in cases of serious disagreement, what the inventory manager decides will usually stick.

Position confers authority to act within a certain scope but not beyond it. The inventory manager, for example, may reign within her defined domain but has no authority to act in others, such as marketing or finance. She can advise or share her judgment but not command in those areas.

Position also confers control over specific resources. For example, the safety manager for a commercial airline can keep a scheduled flight at the gate if conditions, in his opinion, warrant it. Even the CEO may be unwilling to overrule the safety manager's decisions.

It is tempting to rely on positional power and its authority to motivate behavior and get work done: "I'm the boss, and this is what you must do." This is a particular temptation for newly minted supervisors and managers who have not yet identified or developed other sources of power. Those who lean heavily on the authority of their positions, however, may be surprised when that power fails to enlist the collaboration of subordinates. In many cases, subordinates resent being ordered around and respond with poorly done work or work done at a glacial pace.

In an era when people are accustomed to challenging authority, pulling rank is seldom an effective use of power. Harvard professor John Kotter points to two reasons. The first is that managers are dependent on many people—including their own subordinates. Second, "virtually no one in modern organizations will passively accept and completely obey a constant stream of orders from someone just because he or she is the 'boss.'"[1]

Whether or not you use it, the power of position is highly visible to subordinates. It is always in the "on" position and will always set you apart from your subordinates, who are very aware of your power over their livelihoods. One manager interviewed for this book put it this way:

> Subordinates see you as a member of a different caste, and as a person capable of helping or hurting them. This means that you must be careful in how you speak with subordinates. They listen carefully for clues to your moods and intentions, which are bound to affect them. Even remarks made in jest can have an unintended impact. For example, you may joke, "Well, if this project doesn't work, some people will have to walk the plank." That type of light-hearted remark reminds subordinates that you have the power to eliminate their jobs and incomes.

Another manager had this to say: "Like it or not, power differences between people determine their relationships. As a manager, you might want to maintain friendly relationships with subordinates. But forget about being friends. As long as you have the power to appraise their performance and to advance or retard their careers, you cannot be friends in the normal sense."

Here are a few tips for making the most of the power of position:

- Invoke positional power only when absolutely necessary. Recognize that few objectives can be accomplished through positional power alone. As a manager you depend on the help of other departments and your own subordinates to get jobs done. So use persuasion and other means whenever possible to get what you want.

- Be sure that you understand the boundaries of your positional power; don't try to apply it beyond those boundaries. For example, if you are the corporate counsel, invoke your authority on all legal matters but not on matters related to marketing or finance, areas where others have legitimate positional power.

- Defend your positional power from encroachment by others. Ambitious managers are always looking for ways to increase their power. Don't allow them to do so at your expense. For example, if your boss begins to meet separately with your direct reports to assign work or evaluate their performance, have a talk with your boss about lines of authority. His usurping of your authority and responsibilities will undermine your positional power and reduce your ability to achieve the goals he has assigned to you.

Relational Power

Relational power is an informal power that emerges from your relationships with others. For example, a mentor has relationship power that she can use to influence the behavior of a protégé. A coalition is yet another example of relational power, and one that effective managers rely on when units must collaborate to get things done. Managers with very little positional power, for example, can wield substantial power if they are successful in forming collaborative relationships.

Another form of relational power is based on coalitions, dependencies, and what some call the law of reciprocity. Let's consider
each of these power sources and discuss what you can do to increase
them.

Building Power Through Coalitions

Coalitions enable weaker parties to gather the power needed to push
through their proposals or to block those they find unacceptable. As
"Solidarity Forever," an old labor union anthem from the 1940s tells
us, nothing is weaker than the strength of one; collective action, in
contrast, makes us strong. Coalitions are common in labor relations,
politics, international diplomacy, and war. They are also eminently
useful in business.

There are two types of coalitions you should understand: a *natural coalition* of allies who share a broad range of common interests,
and a *single-issue coalition,* in which parties that differ on other issues
unite to support or block a single issue (often for different reasons).

A natural coalition of allies is usually long-lasting because its
members share fundamental interests of substantial breadth. They
see eye to eye on a range of issues. For example, a product development team and the head of corporate sales may share a common goal
and act in concert when financial analysts attempt to block development of a new product line they deem important. These parties also
have a common interest in projects that result in incremental improvement in existing products. Because of their broad basis of mutual interests, natural coalitions are difficult to break.

A single-issue coalition of otherwise disassociated parties, in
contrast, is generally less powerful because (1) the basis for collaboration is more limited, and (2) the coalition forms around a fleeting
issue. Consequently, the single-issue coalition is less long-lasting and
easier to defeat, especially if the other side can divide and conquer.
For example, a labor union and a nature conservation group might
form a coalition to block an anti-union developer from building a
shopping mall in a wooded area. Each party has its own reasons for
joining the blocking coalition, and that makes it possible for the

other side to put a wedge between them. If the property owner finds a different developer with a better track record in dealing with unions, the union is likely to withdraw its opposition to the shopping mall, leaving the conservationists to fight alone. Or if the developer agrees to take steps to minimize the mall's environmental impact, the conservation group is likely to pull out, leaving the union as the sole opponent.

You can boost your relational power by joining coalitions of other employees who have broad, common agendas. Take a moment right now to do the following:

- Ask yourself, What workplace issues would I be more successful in managing if I were part of a like-minded coalition?

- If a coalition is a feasible approach to exerting power on those issues, which individuals or departments would be logical and reliable allies?

If joining a coalition is a feasible approach, go for it. But don't be a passive participant. You will enhance your relational power in the company if you demonstrate leadership, trustworthiness, and a concern for the interests of your coalition partners.

Dependencies

Dependencies are a natural part of human society. We depend on other people for some things, and they depend on us for others. We see an explicit manifestation of dependencies in the everyday life of medieval Europe, where relationships and obligations were carefully codified. In pre-Norman England, for example, every freeman was dependent on the local thane, a minor gentry, for protection during times of trouble. The thane maintained a fortified house for that purpose. The thane in turn depended on the labor of each local freeman and on a portion of his crops. Lacking that support, the thane could not support his fortress, his weaponry, or his retainers. The thane was bound up in yet another dependence, this one involving his superior, the earl. The thane looked to the earl for protection and for the administration of justice, and the earl depended on military service by each of his thanes and their retainers during times of war. This set of dependencies served medieval people fairly well. Everyone gave something, and everyone got something in return. Of course, the people at the top were served best of all.

Similarly, complex organizations are bound up in mutual dependencies. Market researchers, for example, are dependent on field data gathered by the company's sales representatives and by funding provided by the marketing department. The marketing department, in turn, depends heavily on the quality of information provided by market researchers and by product inventories made available by the production department. Every functional area of a business organization can point to dozens of functional dependencies. These exist within departments and also across departmental lines. None of these dependencies is a part of anyone's formal job description. They do not appear in any organization chart. Yet every one of them is an element of relational power for someone.

What are your dependencies? All new managers are surprised by how much they depend on others to get things done. These dependencies constrain managers' options. They cannot easily command people who could retaliate by withholding something of value.

Logically, your net power from dependency relationships is a function of two factors: (1) the dependence of other people on you (a positive factor) and (2) the extent to which you are dependent on others (a negative factor). Thus, you can increase your relational power by reducing your dependence on others or by making others more dependent on you (or both).

To better understand your dependency relationships, make a list similar to the one in figure 2-1, which indicates the dependency relationships of Roland, a district sales manager. Identify the people or departments on which you depend (and for what), and do the same for the people or departments that depend on you. This assessment will give you a capsule view of your dependencies and will suggest avenues for creating a more favorable situation—one that will increase your net power.

FIGURE 2-1

Roland's Workplace Dependencies

I depend on . . .	For . . .
Lisa (clerical assistant)	Handling details of our sales conferences
David (production)	Coordinating sales efforts with the production department
Carlos (finance)	Keeping me up-to-date on budget variances
Joan (information systems)	Weekly sales figures for the company and for my sales reps
Doris, Jean, Arnold, Max, Truman (my sales reps)	Meeting annual sales quota and for passing on field intelligence with respect to customers, competitors, and products

. . . depends on me	For . . .
Gwen (inventory control)	Timely information on near-term sales
Don (subordinate)	Career-enhancing assignments
Karl (accounts receivable)	Dealing with customers whose accounts are past due
Doris, Jean, Arnold, Max, Truman (my sales reps)	Positive performance evaluations, assistance in closing key sales, my permission to be flexible on price or terms in special cases, etc.

As you look for power-altering possibilities, consider the nature of your dependencies on others. How deep are they? Most will be benign, but others may constrain your freedom of action and thus weaken your ability to manage activities for which you have responsibility. A good example in figure 2-1 may be Roland's dependence on Joan, the information systems manager, for timely sales data. Information is a source of power in every modern organization, and some IS managers hoard that power by keeping a tight grip on the gathering and dissemination of information. "Joan keeps our sales data bottled up," Roland complains. "I have to beg for that data and rarely have it when I need it most."

Roland's dependence on Joan is not conducive to his effectiveness as a manager. He should take steps to reduce or eliminate this dependence, perhaps by moving sales data gathering and storage into the sales and marketing department, where he would have more immediate access. Doing so would increase his net power, all other things remaining the same.

After you've analyzed your dependencies on others, turn to the relationships in which others depend on you. Each of these relationships is a positive power factor from your perspective, and that power helps you be effective. For example, Karl, the accounts receivable manager, depends to some extent on Roland for help in collecting from customers whose bills are overdue. Karl will say periodically, "Roland, Gizmo Corporation is already three weeks overdue on its bill. Could you give your contact there a call and encourage them to send us a check?" Roland knows that his personal intervention with overdue customers will help Karl with his responsibility: to collect all receivables in a timely way. Roland also knows that Karl's dependence has from time to time given him some negotiating power with the finance department when customers need special terms in financing their purchases. Deeper dependence by Karl might give Roland even greater negotiating power and a freer hand in recruiting new customers.

Take a minute to think about your dependency relationships. In particular, think about these two things:

- How you can either reduce or eliminate your power-robbing dependencies on others

- How you can increase power-enhancing dependencies of others on you

The Law of Reciprocity

Relational power can also be increased through a system of reciprocity. Whenever you do a favor for someone else, a change takes place in the relationship. The other person owes you a favor in return. This is the *law of reciprocity*, which demands that every favor must someday be repaid. Whoever invented our society must have been an accountant, because much of what goes on is based on personal favors payable and receivable. We know instinctively that doing a favor for someone else creates an obligation to return that favor in some way sometime in the future. The favor is registered in the "accounts receivable" section of our personal balance sheet. A person

Handling Your Dependency on Your Boss

You depend on your boss for many things: resources, information, and occasional support. Given these dependencies, maintaining a good relationship with your boss is very important. But what is the best way to handle it? In his book *Power and Influence,* Harvard professor John Kotter made these observations about successful subordinates.

- They learn about the boss's goals, strengths, weaknesses, and working style.

- They learn the same about themselves.

- They use what they've learned to create a relationship that satisfies both the boss and themselves.

Successful subordinates also work at maintaining a good relationship by being honest, keeping the boss informed, and being dependable in their work.

SOURCE: John P. Kotter, *Power and Influence* (New York: Free Press, 1985), 100–101.

who has many receivables has future money in the bank, so to speak, and this provides some level of power.

Readers of Mario Puzo's bestselling novel *The Godfather* will recall how Don Vito Corleone managed to build his power, in part, by doing favors for people in his community. Those favors obliged their recipients to do things for the don when he needed help. The favors he did over the years—both legal and illegal—were one base of Corleone's power in the community. In this the don was merely following the example of the political dons of America's eastern cities of the late nineteenth century. These political bosses got their poor and powerless constituents out of scraps with landlords and the police. They helped them locate apartments and found places for them on the city payroll. Those many favors were the source of the bosses' power on election day, when the debts were called. Debtors wouldn't be asked simply to vote but also to campaign in their neighborhoods for the political boss, to get people to the polls, and—in some instances—to cast more than one ballot. Reciprocity was the name of the game.

What does your balance sheet of favors look like? Are you a net debtor or, like Don Corleone, a substantial creditor? If you are a substantial creditor—if you have a large balance of "receivable" favors—take care that your generosity is not being exploited by people who have no intention of repaying it. Like a credit manager, you should determine which individuals have the capacity *and* the intention of reciprocating. You can make that determination by asking for a favor in return.

One of the interesting features of relational power is its independence from the formal power associated with your place in the organization. Thus, middle managers and staff personnel are capable of wielding power based on the many favors they have done for others (the law of reciprocity) and the extent to which more highly placed people depend on them. They may also find a source of power within coalitions.

Relationships are an important source of power, but you must be judicious in using them. Managers must sense when to tap these relationships and avoid overexploiting them.

Personal Power

The final source of power that bears mentioning is *personal power.* Personal power is the power you have after the powers of position and relationships are stripped away. It is a function of one or many qualities that others recognize in you. In most cases these include the following:

- Trustworthiness

- Relating well to others

- Expertise of high value to others

- An ability to communicate opinions and ideas in compelling ways

- Accomplishments that merit admiration and respect

- A charismatic style that engages the emotions and allegiance of others

- Powerful and attractive ideas

- Enthusiasm and dedication to hard work

- An ability to enlist collaboration among fellow employees

- Self-confidence

- Abundant physical energy and stamina

The sum of these personal qualities is a measure of your personal power. That power makes it possible to lead in the absence of formal authority and to influence the thinking and behavior of others over whom you have no organizational control. Consider the following example:

> Hard work and expertise in flexible manufacturing helped Philip gain substantial recognition within SupplyCo, an electronic components manufacturer. The idea of integrating data systems, computer-controlled equipment, and production processes was new and radical when he joined the company in 1985. But Philip had the technical know-how and foresight to recognize its potential. He also had the interpersonal skills to make a winning case for its adoption as SupplyCo's new manufacturing strategy, which he helped implement. That strategy was highly successful, giving SupplyCo a competitive advantage.
>
> After flexible manufacturing was solidly rooted, Philip began beating the drum for a related initiative: digital links between SupplyCo and its industrial customers. "We can serve our customers faster and better if we integrate our information systems with theirs," he told anyone who would listen. "This will help both them and us to eliminate costly inventories." And because of Philip's reputation as an idea man, people listened.

Do you have people like Philip in your company? How are they regarded by the people above and below them in the hierarchy? People like Philip generate considerable respect and attention based on the personal power they earn through hard work, forward thinking, regular contributions, and their ability to communicate ideas that interest others. They aren't always highly placed—indeed, they may not have much of a knack for managing—but their opinions are respected. These are the individuals to whom others turn for advice, information, and even direction. Consequently, they are given a place at the table when important matters are being discussed.

We need look no further than the late W. Edwards Deming, a leader of the quality movement of the 1970s and 1980s, to find an individual whose remarkable personal power made him an industrial legend. Deming embodied most of the personal qualities just listed. Although he practiced as a solo consultant and gained widespread notice in the United States only when he was well past normal retirement age, Deming's personal power changed the thinking and behavior of major corporations on four continents.

Deming (1900–1993) learned the principles of statistical process control (SPC) while working at AT&T during the 1930s with pioneering statistician Walter Shewhart. During World War II, Deming taught those principles to American manufacturing managers, helping them ensure quality, reduce waste, and save resources as they produced military equipment and munitions. After the war, Deming was invited by the Union of Japanese Scientists and Engineers (JUSE) to instruct its members in SPC principles. With their industrial infrastructure flattened by Allied bombing, the Japanese were open to ideas that would get their economy back on its feet.

Japanese managers and engineers were very swayed by their American visitor, who was viewed as highly trustworthy because he told them to ignore "misguided" American manufacturing methods and to adopt others. They also respected Deming's expertise in the techniques of quality control and recognized that his ideas could transform and revitalize their war-torn industries.

By the early 1950s, quality had become the religion of Japanese industry, and Deming was its high priest. JUSE established the annual

Personal Power and Informal Leadership

Chances are that you encounter many situations in which you must lead and manage when you are not the boss—that is, when you do not have the formal authority that comes with a position. This is commonplace in organizations that manage work through cross-functional teams. The team leader may be out-ranked by one or more team members. This is the time personal power truly matters. To learn more about leading when you're not the boss, read appendix A, which offers a five-step approach to this challenge.

Deming Prize, which, even today, honors corporations that best adhere to Deming's principles.[2] By the late 1970s, the power of Deming's ideas enjoyed a renaissance in his home country, making him one of the most sought-after lecturers and consultants to top management.

Deming exemplifies how an individual without organizational authority or material resources can influence others and shape the course of events. Chances are that you know of other people like him. What personal qualities account for their power? Do you share any of those qualities?

Rate Yourself

What is your personal power profile? Table 2-1 lists qualities generally associated with personal power. Rate yourself against each one. Then have one or two objective colleagues who know you well do the same. The combined ratings will give you a good idea of your strengths and weaknesses. If you eliminate those weaknesses you will increase your personal power.

Where Is the Power in Your Organization?

To deal effectively with power, you must understand the power that you and others in the organization have. Like electricity, power is

TABLE 2-1

Your Personal Power Profile

Power Trait	Below Average	Average	Above Average
Trustworthiness. Speaks the truth.			
Ability to relate well with others. Understands the value of give and take.			
Expertise that others value. Has knowledge or technical expertise that can translate into business success.			
Communication skills. Can communicate views and ideas in compelling ways.			
Accomplishments. Makes contributions that merit admiration and respect.			
Personal charisma. A style that engages the emotions and allegiance of others.			
Powerful and attractive ideas. Always thinking ahead of the pack.			
Focus and enthusiasm. Not easily diverted or discouraged.			
A welcome member of everyone's team. An ability to enlist collaboration among fellow employees.			
Self-confidence. Not shy about speaking up on important matters.			
Energy and endurance. Tireless in pursuit of key goals.			
Reliable. Always does what he says he will do. Can be counted on to have done his homework.			
Total in each category			

invisible, but you can feel and observe its effects. Start with yourself. What are your sources of power? Are they formal or informal? For example, does your title or position impart any special power? Who is dependent on you? How many well-positioned peers, superiors, or subordinates owe you a debt? What resources do you control? Are you boosting your power through membership in a coalition? Do your personal powers (of communication, visibility, accomplishments, and so on) afford you special power? Is your power greater or less than others with whom you are dealing?

Apply the same analysis to those with whom you interact—those above and below you in the chain of command as well as people in other functions who are outside the chain of command. If you're a long-term employee, you can probably point to the people and the departments that have the most power. If you cannot, or if you're new to the company, look for power in these places:[3]

- Departments or business units whose leaders have the highest salaries or that pay the highest salaries to newcomers. Salary size is usually a useful indicator of what top management and the board of directors value.

- Departments or business units that have the most representation in top management and on the board of directors. For example, some companies reflexively look to finance or the sales organization for their next CEO. In contrast, one would be hard-pressed to find a major organization that ever gave the top job to someone in human resources; that's not where the power is.

- The executive conference room. When key decisions about strategy and resource allocation are made, who's at the table?

- Physical proximity to the CEO's office. The old notion of the palace court continues in our business organizations. People with power usually have offices in the headquarters building close to the top executive's piece of personal real estate.

You can make a rough measurement of your own power, or your boss's power, by simply checking these power indicators.

You now understand the three main sources of power in organizations: power of position, relational power, and personal power. Understanding these will put you in a much better position to tap in to the power you need to get things done.

Summing Up

- The power or authority associated with formal position in the organization is observable at every level. It confers authority to act within a certain scope but is seldom sufficient to get things done.

- Relational power is informal power that emerges from your relationships with others. Some of these relationships represent dependencies, which can either enhance or limit your power.

- If you do a favor for someone else, a change takes place in your relationship with that person, who now owes you a favor in return. This is the law of reciprocity at work, and it impacts relational power.

- Coalitions can increase your relational power.

- Personal power is a function of one or many qualities: ideas, expertise, accomplishments, charisma, communication skill, and trustworthiness. These qualities impart power even when other forms of power are limited.

- You should understand where power resides in the organization. Salary size is usually an indicator.

3

Influence

Your Mechanism for Using Power

Key Topics Covered in This Chapter

- *Influence as a mechanism for using power*

- *Why influence is a two-way street*

- *Enlarging your sphere of influence*

- *Using "currency" exchanges to build influence*

LIKE ELECTRICAL POWER, organizational power is only a potential. Real power is realized only through some form of expression. In organizations, power often expresses itself as influence: the ability to change, direct, or affect the behavior of others without ordering or threatening them.

Power created and held for its own sake is without value; individuals may hope to use it for self-protection or to serve their own ambitions, but power has value for the organization only when it is used to accomplish legitimate goals. This chapter describes the limitations of direct power and explains how managers can use their power indirectly to influence the outcomes they seek.

Power Versus Influence

As described earlier, power is the potential to mobilize resources and to influence others. In her book *Exercising Influence,* Kim Barnes makes the case that power is something you have, whereas influence is something you do.[1] For example, your boss has the power to give you a pay raise, a promotion, and a termination letter. The boss will use that power to influence the direction and quality of your day-to-day work. This supports the notion that power is purely a potential that must be tapped in some way to produce a desired outcome.

We define *influence* as the mechanism through which people use power to change behavior or attitudes. Unlike power, influence can produce an effect without the apparent exertion of force, compulsion, or direct command. In some cases, power can and must be expressed directly, as in the following situations:

- Controlling the allocation of resources

- Settling disputes

- Hiring, firing, and promoting individual employees

- Making assignments

The direct application of power, however, has two important drawbacks. The first and perhaps the most notable of these is that the people on the receiving end of power may respond half-heartedly. The use of direct power circumvents the process of mutual agreement, involvement, and buy-in that normally produces employee commitment and good work in many workplace situations. Unless they are already committed to a project or goal, people directed by power alone will do their work with simmering discontent. People who labor under the heel of direct power must be supervised closely. If the power in question lacks legitimacy, they may even rebel.

The second drawback of applying power directly is that doing so will eventually drain the power "battery." If you accept the analogy of a power battery, you must accept the idea that executives or managers who rely repeatedly on direct power to get things done will eventually dissipate their supply of power, barring a recharging of the power battery. This means that power must be expended judiciously and only for the most important purposes. The application of power through influence demands less of the power supply and is less likely to drain the battery.

Still, there are occasions when directly applied power is accepted, even welcomed. Perhaps the best of these occasions is during a crisis. During a crisis, the subtleties of consensus building, employee empowerment, and group decision making are often jettisoned because they are too slow or too uncertain. People caught in a crisis that threatens their well-being actually welcome a leader—a tough-minded commander—who will take charge, make decisions, and direct their activities.

Democratic nations at war provide clear examples of how people respond positively to greater concentration of power at the top. Consider the experience of the United States, a country that prides itself on its separation of powers, its Bill of Rights, and its checks on governmental power over individuals. During the Civil War (1861–1865), World War II (1941–1945), and the current "war on terror," certain important powers shifted to the chief executive, and various individual protections were compromised in favor of the protection of society in general. Advocates of civil liberties squawked and constitutional scholars complained, but the general public seemed comfortable with these changes. Most people wanted the government to have more power and to use it against foreign and internal enemies.

Even in times of crisis, however, effective leaders understand that they can enhance their success by applying power indirectly—that is, through influence. Here are a few examples of influence through indirectly applied power:

- Framing the issues of an important debate

- Encouraging people to identify with organizational goals

- Enlisting collaboration between cross-functional units

- Encouraging high standards

Any of the sources of power cited earlier—positional power, relational power, or personal power—can be applied to these forms of influence. In each case, however, the intended outcome is basically the same: to encourage other people to do what you want them to do but through *their own choice*. This is reminiscent of the famous episode in Mark Twain's *Tom Sawyer*, in which Tom successfully convinces some other boys that painting his Aunt Polly's fence is so much fun, and such an honor, that they insist on taking over the chore for themselves—and even pay Tom for the privilege.

Let's consider the first of the examples cited earlier to illustrate how a person can apply power indirectly through influence.

Influence Is a Two-Way Street

When you think about influence, think of it as a two-way street. To influence effectively, a manager must be open to influence by others, as shown in figure 3-1. People who influence without subjecting themselves to influence in the process are simply applying direct power.

We suspect that executives and managers who are open to influence by their peers and subordinates are more respected and more influential—and more successful—than those who are resistant to influence. Openness to influence from others, even from subordinates, has two important consequences. First, it is a visible gesture of trust and respect. To gain trust and respect, you must extend it to others. Second, openness is a means of acquiring information and insights about the operational environment. People who resist influence close themselves off from signals about that environment and risk being blindsided by unfolding events.

A good example is found in the story of how senior executives of General Motors in the early 1980s failed to be influenced by their own quality and reliability managers. Those managers tried to convince their bosses through empirical data that Japanese automakers were rapidly outpacing GM on quality issues that mattered to customers. Their case fell on deaf ears—at least for another two years.

FIGURE 3-1

Influence Works Two Ways

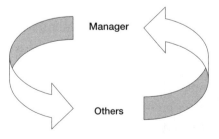

Manager

Others

The top people clearly could influence their Q&R people but seemed immune to influence from Q&R.[2]

Openness to influence begins with being an active listener. Active listening helps you capture what the other side has to say while signaling that you are alert and eager to hear it. Here are some tips for being an active listener:

- Keep your eyes on the speaker.

- Take notes as appropriate.

- Resist the urge to formulate your response as the other person is talking. Give the speaker and argument your full attention.

- Pay attention to the speaker's body language. Body language is often as revealing of the other person's feelings as are words.

- Ask questions to get more information and to encourage the speaker to continue. Questions also indicate that you are paying attention and interested in what the other person has to say.

- Repeat in your own words what you've heard to ensure that you understand and to let the speaker know that you've processed his or her words: "So, you're saying that . . ." However, avoid too much of this repetition, which can be annoying.

You can also demonstrate openness to influence by using open-ended questions in your dialogue with other people. Open-ended questions are those that cannot be answered with a simple yes or no. For example, avoid saying, "That's an interesting idea. Do you think it will solve our problems?" This question invites a yes or no answer, neither of which will provide valuable information. Instead, say something like this: "That's an interesting idea. How will it solve our problem?" Or, "That's an interesting idea. What have others said about it?" These open-ended questions invite the other person to express the idea more completely and provide you with more information.

But being open to influence requires more than lending an open ear to the opinions and ideas of others. You must translate those opinions and ideas—the good ones—into action. If all you do is listen to others and then do exactly what you intended to do, you are not demonstrating that you take them seriously—or are open to influence. People respect and have confidence in leaders and managers who take their ideas seriously; and that respect and confidence naturally make them open to influence by these same leaders and managers. However, people quickly lose respect and confidence in those who ask for their ideas but never take them to heart.

Your Sphere of Influence

Most of us are familiar with the concept of *sphere of influence*: the domain in which one can effectively exert influence. In geopolitics, a nation's sphere of influence is a physical area within which the nation has a high level of, if not dominant, political influence. Thus, Latin America and the Caribbean have traditionally been within the sphere of influence of the United States. Southeast Asia and North Korea fall within China's sphere of influence.

The influence of these two powers is strongest among their closest neighbors and among those with whom each has ideological, language, and commercial ties. Their influence is also strong over countries that depend on these more powerful nations for military, political, or financial support. Their influence is less strong among countries that are either distant or lacking in those ties. We generally conceptualize spheres of influence as a set of concentric circles in which influence is strongest near the center and weaker as the distance from the center increases, as in figure 3-2.

During the Cold War, each of the two rival superpowers—the United States and the Soviet Union—sought to strengthen and extend its sphere of influence. Each, for example, attempted to install or prop up local regimes friendly to its goals. For example, the Soviets, working through communist parties in the so-called Eastern Bloc nations, had substantial control over the top leadership of those client states. The United States did something similar in parts of Latin America and Africa. When U.S. influence in Chile was ended through the election of a communist government, U.S. operatives

FIGURE 3-2

Spheres of Influence

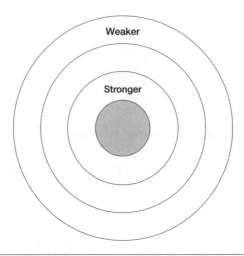

provided backing for the rebels who eventually toppled that government and reestablished friendly ties with the United States.

In other cases, the rival superpowers used economic and military aid to extend their influence. The Soviet Union, for example, attempted to gain a foothold of influence in the Middle East by supplying Egypt with military equipment, technical assistance, and resources for its giant Aswan Dam project. In business organizations, people behave similarly. For example, a manager intent on expanding her influence may promote or hire "her people" for key posts and give them substantial resources. Their loyalty to her assures the manager of a high level of influence.

As in geopolitics, your personal influence is likely to be strong in some spheres and weak in others. The strength of personal influence is generally a function of two elements described in an earlier chapter: one or another form of power, and the level of the dependencies of others. Consider the following two examples:

Caroline has organizational authority over her production department. In addition, her reputation for success and for generating good ideas has given her leverage with the finance department, which controls corporate resources. Whenever her department needs more money in its budget, the CFO will give her a hearing—if not the money—because of the returns she has produced from other funding.

Daniel is a corporate space manager. His job is to provide office space and furnishings for each department of the company. Outside his own small staff, he has no command authority. Nevertheless, Daniel has broad influence in the company. The managers of every department depend on him to provide the floor space they need to do their work, and they go out of their way to maintain good relations with him.

Both Caroline and Daniel have spheres of influence that extend beyond the boundaries of their formal authority. Caroline's external influence is based upon her exemplary performance; Daniel's is based on his control of an important resource on which others depend.

Take a moment to map out your own sphere of influence. Where is it strongest, beginning with the sphere of your formal authority? In what important arenas is it weak? Obviously, your ability to influence people and events is heavily dependent on this sphere of influence. So if you want to be more influential, you must find ways to expand or strengthen your sphere. You can do that by

- increasing your power—either positional, relational, or personal

- finding ways to project your power into areas that are strategically important to you

- creating deeper or more broad-based dependencies by others

- being open to influence by others.

Be strategic in your efforts to extend your influence, giving priority to the spheres that are most relevant to your success. For example, if you're a logistics manager, it is surely more critical to your success to build your influence with your production and marketing departments and with key shipping companies than to extend your influence to others. So as you diagnose your sphere of influence, answer this question: *Where* is my influence most needed? After you've answered that question, you must find a way to create that influence. The next chapter can help.

Increasing Influence Through Currencies of Exchange

In their popular 1989 book, *Influence Without Authority,* scholars Allan Cohen and David Bradford introduced the metaphor of *currencies of exchange* to help business people understand how they can acquire and expand their organizational influence. Currencies, in the view of these authors, are the coinage of influence; they are the resources—goods and services—that can be offered to a potential ally in exchange for cooperation. "Because they represent resources that can be exchanged," Cohen and Bradford write, "currencies are the basis for acquiring influence. If you have no currencies in your treasury, you do not have anything to exchange for what you want."[3]

Think for a moment about the currencies you have at your disposal—the goods and services you can use to build influence with your superiors, peers, and subordinates. For your boss, you might offer your help in developing the PowerPoint slide she needs for an upcoming presentation to senior management, or you might simply provide information she can use in making a winning case. For a peer, a favor such as the free use of your laboratory space might be much appreciated currency. For a subordinate, a challenging new assignment or public recognition of his achievements might be a highly valued currency. No matter what tangible good or intangible service you provide to someone else, the fact that the person values it provides you with some level of influence.

The key to using currencies effectively is to understand what other people want and value. You gain that understanding when you move beyond a superficial level of knowing what motivates, inspires, and concerns people. What really matters to them? What are they trying to accomplish in their careers? What threatens them or stands in the way of their success? How does their view of the world and the organization differ from yours? If you answer these deeper questions, you will be much better positioned to make exchanges and influence the people with whom you do business.

Summing Up

- Influence is a mechanism through which people use power to change behavior or attitudes. Unlike power, influence can produce an effect without the apparent exertion of force, compulsion, or direct command.

- To have influence on others, you must be open to influence from them.

- Active listening and the use of open-ended questions are techniques you can use to demonstrate openness to influence.

- The strength of your personal influence is generally a function of two elements: one or another form of power (positional, relational, or personal) and the level of the dependencies of others.

- You can use the currencies (goods and services) at your disposal to build influence with others in the organization. These currencies may take the forms of technical assistance, information, the lending of space or equipment, a plum assignment, and so forth.

- The key to using currencies is to understand what others want or value.

Tactics of Influence

Three Ways to Project Influence

Key Topics Covered in This Chapter

- *Framing the issue to influence the outcome*

- *Using information to influence thinking and outcomes*

- *How growing complexity gives technical experts greater influence*

N ow that you've learned the general concepts of influence, it's time to think about tactics for translating power into influence. This chapter examines three of these tactics: influence through framing, information, and technical authority. Each is a practical mechanism for influencing others.

Frame the Issue Your Way

A frame is a mental window through which we view reality or a particular problem. For example, twenty years ago concerns about the existence of nuclear weapons were framed in terms of a possible missile exchange between the world's two superpowers: the United States and the Soviet Union. Such an exchange could be triggered by an insane person working in a missile silo or by an erroneous radar report that the other side had already launched its rockets. Some people worried that one side or the other would make a preemptive strike. Today, however, people frame the issue of nuclear weapons much differently; they now worry about the prospects of rogue nations or shadowy terrorist groups getting their hands on these lethal weapons.

Unless we make a concerted effort to do otherwise, we frame reality in terms of our key concerns, interests, closely held beliefs, and prejudices. Thus, a dermatologist who meets someone for the first time is likely to observe a patch of sun-damaged skin on that person's forehead—something the rest of us wouldn't notice. When we walk into a gathering of economically successful people, we are likely to see opportunities to make new acquaintances and learn something new about personal success. A real estate salesperson walking into the same gathering is likely to see a roomful of potential homebuyers and sellers. The well-worn expression "If you're a hammer, everything looks like a nail" is a humorous way to describe the power of framing from an individual perspective.

Framing the issue or the agenda for others is a powerful approach to exerting influence. As Jeffrey Pfeffer has written in *Managing With Power,* "Establishing the framework within which issues will be viewed and decided is often tantamount to determining the result."[1] Consider this example:

> *A group of publishing executives had convened to discuss a proposal offered by David, one of their company's managers. David had proposed that the company acquire the rights to a ten-volume self-paced learning course that was currently being used to prepare newly hired securities salespeople for their licensing examination. The publication was not like anything the company had previously published, and it would involve direct selling to end customers instead of selling through book wholesalers and retailers.*
>
> *The senior financial person at the table quizzed David about the projected revenues and costs of manufacturing and distribution. He was far from enthusiastic. "Based on your projections, this project would have a positive net present value, but just barely," he said. "And the rate of return is below what we demand of new projects."*
>
> *The marketing executive picked up where the first interrogator left off, asking for more details about unit sales prices and David's method for generating his revenue projections.*
>
> *David could see that the meeting was going to be a dull and predictable evaluation of the project, using revenues and costs as the frame of reference. Unless he acted quickly, the novelty of the publication for this company, and its potential impact on the company's future growth, would be absent from the discussion.*
>
> *To everyone's surprise, David didn't respond to the numbers issues. He politely deflected the first round of questions and launched into*

something unanticipated. "This proposal isn't about the profits of a single project," he began. "It's about an opportunity to break out of the rut we've been in for the past ten years by entering a new market—a market with fat profit margins and major growth potential. It's about an opportunity to sell directly to our customers instead of through the wholesalers and national book chains who take most of the profits out of our work and our products."

The assembled executives were slightly stunned but now attentive. David had hit two important hot buttons: fat profit margins and major growth. So they gave him the floor. "Whether this particular product makes money or loses money is much less important than the publishing opportunities we are likely to find once we gain a beachhead in that new market," David said. He made an analogy to his project and the Normandy invasion during World War II. "By traditional measures, the first day of the invasion was a costly loss. If people simply calculated the gains and losses of that one day, they would have to say, 'We should have stayed in England.' But that single day opened the door to a larger victory."

After a pause, the executives resumed their questions. But their questions were no longer about short-term sales and expense projections; instead, they were about how David's project might help the company grow and become more profitable.

In this example, David decisively reframed the discussion—a useful tactic for exerting influence. What gave him the power to do this? It wasn't formal, positional power, because he was clearly outranked by the executives in the room. Perhaps it was David's personal power—his record of accomplishment, his recognized expertise, or the power of his ideas—that allowed him to reframe the discussion.

Take a moment to think about workplace issues that are important to you. Are they being approached within the right framework? If they are not, how can you use your influence to reframe those issues? Can you apply positional power or relational power to make it happen? What elements of personal power can you draw on to reframe people's thinking? Also think about how you can influence others to identify with organizational goals, to collaborate, and to adopt high standards.

If you get people to look at issues in a different way, you will have influenced them through framing.

Influence Through Information

It is often possible to influence people and the direction of debate through the presentation of compelling and irrefutable facts and numbers. Consider the following case:

In 2002 through 2004, two organized groups of citizens were locked in a debate over the future of their town's remaining piece of undisturbed forestland. A group of golfing enthusiasts wanted to expand the existing and adjacent nine-hole municipal course into that forest, creating an eighteen-hole course. "The existing course is a huge money-maker," they proclaimed. They cited $250,000 in annual profits from the existing course and spoke of the many municipal amenities those earnings made possible for the community: a sailing program for kids, computers for the high school, and so forth. "Doubling the size of the course will bring in even more money for the town—money it desperately needs," they argued. Several town councilors announced their support for the plan, pointing to the need for additional revenues.

Opposing the plan was an alliance of hikers, bird-watchers, and other people who wanted this piece of woodland left undisturbed. They too had political support.

Over many months, each side argued its position and denounced the other. But they were talking past each other, with the golf boosters talking about financial benefits and other side touting the benefits of untrammeled forest—two very different values that could not be directly compared. There was no point around which the two sides—and the community at large—could join the debate and weigh the benefits and environmental costs of the golf course plan. It was an impasse.

The impasse was eventually broken when a private citizen took the time to examine the finances of the existing golf course, something that had never been done. Each of the contending sides had heretofore accepted without question the golf course's profitability figures, as calculated by the town's park superintendent. In his investigation, however,

this citizen discovered that half of the course's operating costs—for
water, employee benefits, fuel, debt payments, and so forth—was coming
from the town's general fund and was not counted in the measurement
of the golf course's profits. By his reckoning, the course was a breakeven
operation. Worse, his figures showed that the cost of building and man-
aging the proposed eighteen-hole course would produce sizable financial
losses for the twenty years during which the construction loan would
have to be paid off.

That new information was presented to the contending sides and to
the town's elected officials. The town newspaper ran a feature on it, as
did the local television news. The new information had a sudden and
decisive influence on the debate. Instead of the issue being new revenues
versus the owls and chipmunks, the debate now crystallized around the
lackluster financial performance of the golf course. Why had it performed
so poorly? Why had the real costs of its operation been hidden? In light
of the facts, political support for the golf course plan melted away. The
forest area not only was spared from the axe but also was given conser-
vation protection.

This true tale demonstrates how information can influence
people and the course of events. In business, that influential information usually takes the form of financial figures. Naturally, the validity of those figures is critical. In their widely read book *Relevance
Lost: The Rise and Fall of Management Accounting,* Thomas Johnson and
Robert Kaplan explain how sloppy cost accounting, as in the golf
course case, gives false signals, encouraging managers to support un-
profitable products and projects even as they shut down their true
sources of value creation.[2] In other cases, advocates use information
selectively, just as an attorney will present all the facts that support
her client while keeping silent about those that do the opposite.
Thus, an individual who develops a reputation for solid objectivity,
rationality, and truthfulness—hallmarks of personal power—can use
information to influence internal debate and key decisions.

So take a moment to consider the important debates raging in your
organization. These may be about creating new products, launching
internal projects, reviewing pricing, building a new facility, or implementing a new strategy. Whatever the case, think about the in-

Information and the Unmaking of a President

To appreciate the power of information in shaping events, we need look no further than the Watergate affair. In June 1972, a bungled burglary at the Watergate offices of the Democratic National Committee set the stage for the biggest political scandal in American history and the abdication of a powerful president. That break-in, which would be revealed to have originated in the Nixon White House, was not a major story when the burglars were first arraigned. And the whole thing might have blown over had it not been for periodic leaks of information from a tipster to two enterprising journalists, whose reporting kept the story alive and eventually turned it into a national issue.

Washington Post reporters Bob Woodward and Carl Bernstein received information from an inside source whose identity, to this day, has never been revealed. This clandestine source, known as Deep Throat, helped the two reporters turn the story of a minor burglary into a national scandal with far-reaching consequences for the country.

formation that could influence those debates. If you can provide accurate, relevant, and objective information on the key issues facing your company, you can influence the debate—and increase your own personal power.

Influence Through Technical Authority

Many important decisions involve technical information over which generalist CEOs and executives have no mastery. Consequently, they look to people with this mastery for guidance, creating opportunities for influence. Consider this example:

> *Fred and Cynthia were co-owners of a small but growing information technology services company. Between the two of them, they knew almost everything about setting up IT systems, Web site development,*

and data storage for the dozens of small client businesses they served. They were prototypical techno-geeks.

Unfortunately, their knowledge did not extend to the many other areas of expertise required by successful, growing businesses. They were clueless about employee benefits, taxes, sources of expansion financing, and other matters. Sensing their own weaknesses, Fred and Cynthia hired George, a young but experienced manager with an M.B.A. degree. He was no digital wizard, but he was knowledgeable in matters of business strategy and operations. Within six months of joining the company, George had made a major mark on the business. He convinced the owners of the merits of abandoning their partnership in favor of a corporate form of business. Working with local bankers, he negotiated a refinancing of the company's debt at better terms and established a line of credit. He also set up a retirement plan for the two owners and participating employees. Even more important, George helped Fred and Cynthia understand the importance of developing a five-year strategy for their business.

As time went by, Fred and Cynthia came to rely more heavily on George's business acumen and advice. George's influence became even stronger as he became more knowledgeable about information technology.

You've undoubtedly experienced situations like this one in your own work, where one individual's technical expertise has given him or her exceptional influence. This may be a modern phenomenon. Three hundred years ago, most of the accumulated knowledge of the Western world was contained in perhaps less than a thousand books. Educated people in the early 1700s drew on the best of that common core of literature, which included the Bible, the works of great philosophers and historians of the ancient world, the luminaries of the Renaissance, and authors of the emerging scientific and political Enlightenment. Anyone who had access to this literature, and the time to read it, could pass as a learned person who had mastered the knowledge of the times.

Today, almost fifty thousand books are published annually in the United States alone, and academic journals have proliferated. Knowledge far exceeds the capacity of even the most brilliant individual. As a result, learning has become highly specialized, and we have become increasingly reliant on specialists and technical experts who, as a cynic might put it, spend their time learning more and more about less and less.

The value of technical expertise is compounded by the complexity of the modern world. Virtually everyone in developed countries has access to computers, synthetic compounds, cell phones, e-mail, and flat-screen displays, and yet few of us can explain how these things work; we certainly cannot make or repair them. Mind-boggling complexity has also invaded the U.S. tax code, which currently covers more than twenty-two thousand pages and is growing every year. To cope, we leave the complexities of these gizmos and the tax system to technical specialists and lean on them for advice.

Our dependence has given these technical specialists substantial influence in business and government. For example, company executives who reached the top through marketing or finance can appreciate the benefits of having a knockout e-commerce site, but they are usually clueless about the details of creating and operating one. What differentiates a powerful site from a weak one? What does it take to build one? Who needs to be part of the building process? What will it cost? Lacking answers, they inevitably turn to technical experts, who, in the end, have substantial influence over the decisions and monetary outlays made at the top by nontechnical executives.

Do you have technical expertise on which company decision makers depend? If you do, think about the many ways you can employ your expertise to influence important decisions. If you lack technical expertise, consider acquiring some through on the-job or formal training.

This discussion of influence is far from exhaustive. However, it suggests some of the principal tactics that people use to influence others. The best lessons, however, can be found in your own organization. So be alert. Watch how the most respected and effective people in your company influence you and others. Use the most effective and ethical of these influencers as your teachers.

Summing Up

- A frame is a mental window through which we view reality or a particular problem. You can influence people's thinking and their decisions by establishing the frame.

- Information is another lever of influence. Just be sure that it is compelling and irrefutable.

- You can use technical authority to increase your influence. Because of the complexity of modern business and everyday life, many people—including key decision makers—have come to rely heavily on the advice and input of technical experts.

Persuasion I

The Basics

Key Topics Covered in This Chapter

- *The necessity of persuasion in management*

- *The four elements of persuasion*

- *Influence mapping as a guide to knowing whom to persuade*

- *Various types of audiences and decision styles*

- *Characteristics of a rock-solid case*

A FEW MONTHS AGO, Margaret was promoted to manager of benefits administration. Last week she read an interesting article about a new benefits program that many other companies like hers are implementing. Margaret believes that implementing this program will save her company money and will generate more choices for employees. She'd like to convince her boss and other key players in the company of the program's value. Although she is certain that the organization would be better off switching to the new program, she recognizes the obstacles ahead of her. The company has a long history with its current benefits program, and some managers and employees may resist her idea. She has some influence over company decision makers, but they all outrank her. What should she do?

Margaret must employ persuasion to achieve her goal. This chapter explains why persuasion is important and introduces its basic elements.[1] But before we begin, try to answer each of the following questions.[2] They will help you assess your current persuasive abilities.

Do you know how to make your arguments interesting to others?

When you attempt to persuade someone, do you effectively adapt your manner of speaking to the type of person you are speaking to?

Do you have a sense of how high to set your goals when trying to change someone's thoughts or actions?

Can you sense the best time to attempt to change someone's mind on an issue of importance to you?

Do you support your ideas with reasons that others find compelling?

For managers—those with power and those without it—persuasion is the primary means of changing behavior and affecting decisions. In this sense, effective persuasion is a form of power and a tool of influence. To persuade is to use argument or entreaty to get others to adopt a belief or particular behavior. Talented persuaders have the power to capture an audience, sway its opinions, and convince opponents to align with their cause.

What exactly is persuasion? *Persuasion* is a process that enables a person or group to change or reinforce others' attitudes, opinions, or behaviors. It can take place in a single meeting or over time through a series of discussions. Persuasion is a skill that's essential for success in all relationships—personal and business alike. What's more, persuasion is not only a matter of making a rational case but also about presenting information and ideas in ways that appeal to fundamental human emotions. It's about positioning an idea, approach, or solution in a way that appeals to others.

Persuasion blends art and science. It's an art in that it requires the ability to establish trust. It's a science in that it is based on the disciplined collection and analysis of information, a solid understanding of human behavior, and well-developed communications skills. By adopting this art and science, anyone can enhance his or her persuasion skills.

Why Persuasion Is Important

The applications of persuasion are virtually infinite. An employee lobbying for a pay raise, a sales manager pitching the benefits of a new product line to a customer, a purchasing manager convincing a supplier to expedite shipment of an order—these are only a few examples of persuasion situations. We draw upon our persuasive skills every day, usually without realizing it.

Changes in the business world have made persuasion a more critical managerial skill than ever. Here are two reasons:

- The days of executive command-and-control have given way to a world increasingly characterized by cross-functional teams of peers, joint ventures, and intercompany partnerships. Command-and-control is absent from this new world, where it is seen as either illegitimate or counterproductive.

- Many people in the work force have grown up questioning authority. They do not respond well to being told what to do; they respond best when persuaded of the logic and benefits of doing things and in particular ways.

Clearly, formal authority no longer gets executives and managers as far as it used to. To do their job—accomplishing work through others—they must persuade others rather than simply issue orders.

The Elements of Persuasion

Persuasion requires preparation and planning. This is something we rarely think about, even though most of us engage in persuasive activity on a daily basis. It also involves four elements:

1. Credibility

2. An understanding of the audience

3. A solid argument

4. Effective communication

We'll treat the first three elements in this chapter and deal with power aspects of communication in chapter 6.

Building Credibility

Credibility is a cornerstone of persuasion. Without it, your audience will dismiss your proposal. Consider the time-honored fable of the child who cried "wolf" too often. This boy sounded the alarm among his rural neighbors whenever he thought that a dangerous wolf was on the prowl. After much commotion, these warnings were found to be baseless, and the boy lost his credibility. When a wolf did appear, no one would listen to him.

Your own credibility manifests itself on two levels:

- **Your ideas.** For you to be credible, your ideas must be perceived as sound. For example, the new product concept you have proposed must make sense in light of current market conditions, technology, and business concerns. Also, you must have thought through all ramifications of the proposal.

- **You as a person.** Other people must view you as believable, trustworthy, and sincere. Generally, these are personal qualities you must earn over time in working with others. Have you demonstrated these personal qualities?

Credibility is generally understood in terms of this simple but powerful formula:

Credibility = Trust + Expertise

The more trust you earn and the more expertise you accumulate, the more credible you *and* your ideas become.

Trust

When people trust you, they are inclined to see you as believable, well informed, and sincere. They know that you will respect their interests and will not act in ways that undermine those interests. They also view you as possessing a strong emotional character (a steady temperament) and integrity (honesty and reliability). Those qualities reinforce your appeal, and that in turn makes people more inclined to accept your ideas. In contrast, people will discount or disregard everything you say if you are viewed as untrustworthy.

Here are several ways to earn people's trust:

- **Tell both sides of the story as you understand it.** If you are proposing something, be candid with people about the pros and cons. For example, in proposing a new venture, give an objective estimate of the best, worst, and most likely outcomes.

- **Deliver on your promises.** Do you always deliver on promises and commitments you've made? If you do, people will notice and consider you to be trustworthy.

- **Keep confidences.** If someone shares information in confidence, respect that confidence unless you are legally or ethically obliged to do otherwise. For example, suppose another manager says, "I'd like your opinion on the landscape design my team has developed for the new office park. The design is very rough at this stage, and we know it has flaws, so I'd appreciate your not sharing it with others for now. Is that okay with you?" If you agree to this confidentiality, then stand by your decision. If you demonstrate that you will respect confidential information, you will develop a reputation for trustworthiness.

- **Be consistent in your values.** Almost everyone can point to friendships and successful working relationships with people whom they disagree with on important issues. Consider the example of the late U.S. President Ronald Reagan, a Republican and staunch political conservative, and the late Speaker of the U.S. House of Representatives, "Tip" O'Neil, a liberal Democrat. The two men were miles apart in their views on the role of government. Nevertheless, they managed to develop a trusting working relationship because each respected the other's consistent adherence to his core values. Each could count on the other to behave in ways that were true to those values.

- **Encourage the exploration of ideas.** Listen to others' concerns in order to encourage dialogue and demonstrate your openness to their perspectives. Establish an environment in which people can share their ideas and know that their opinions are valued. This is much different from an environment in which people are chided and ignored if their views are out of step with those of the boss.

- **Put others' best interests first.** People will trust you and your ideas more if you can demonstrate that you have their interests in mind. For example, suppose a marketing director helps a valued subordinate get promoted to a different department. The marketing director hates to lose a top-notch team member, but she accepts the idea that helping others develop their professional skills is part of her job as a manager. In helping her subordinate, the marketing director earns the trust not only of that one person but also of peers and other subordinates, who tell themselves, "She put the other person's interests ahead of her own."

Trust between people doesn't happen overnight. It is developed only over time and through a series of personal interactions and observed behaviors. So if you behave repeatedly in a trustworthy manner you will earn a reputation for being trustworthy.

Expertise

Like trust, expertise helps you build credibility. People perceive you as having expertise when you exercise sound judgment and demonstrate a history of successes. To build or strengthen your expertise, follow these guidelines:

- **Research your ideas.** Find out everything you can about the idea you are proposing by talking with knowledgeable individuals, reading relevant sources, and so forth. Collect data and information that both support *and* contradict your idea. Doing so will make you well versed on the strengths and weaknesses of your position.

- **Get firsthand experience.** Nothing is as powerful as demonstrating expertise. For example, if you plan to advocate a new
  method of distribution, get out of the office and talk with customers and the people who work in marketing and logistics.
  This experience will help you understand the nuances of distribution that you could never learn from textbooks or second-
  hand sources.

- **Cite trusted sources.** Back your position with knowledge
  gained from respected business or trade periodicals, books,
  independent reports, lectures, and acknowledged experts—
  both inside and outside your organization. It's always smart to
  demonstrate that you are not the only voice supporting a particular point of view.

- **Prove it.** Launch a small pilot project to demonstrate that your
  ideas will work. For example, if you're advocating a new
  process for your department, conduct a limited experiment
  with the process to generate firsthand information about its
  benefits. If your pilots uncover weaknesses, develop practical
  remedies for them.

- **Master the language of your topic.** Workers in most fields develop their own language, including buzzwords. This is true in
  the fields of finance, information systems, investment management, materials management, and countless other endeavors.
  You need to master the language of your field if you want to
  persuade people who work in these fields. So pay close attention to language during meetings, industry conferences, and
  other business gatherings. Make sure that you understand the
  true meaning of that language—and use it appropriately in persuasion communications.

- **Don't hide your credentials.** If appropriate, let people know
  about any experience you have or relevant advanced degrees
  you've earned. For example, a personal trainer who is launching a line of nutritional supplements would want to advertise
  her degree in nutrition alongside her credentials as a licensed

physical therapist. But note that in some companies, publicizing academic credentials is considered bad form. Doing so might hurt your credibility if your colleagues firmly believe that it's a person's ideas that count and not his or her degrees.

- **Team up with credible allies.** Enlist the help of people with established credentials to augment your own expertise. These allies might be other employees with specialized training or experience, an outside consultant, or even a customer. Their standing in the field will bolster your own.

- **Gather endorsements.** People are often swayed by testimonials from respected, authoritative sources. If other departments or companies are currently enjoying success with the practices or products you advocate, then gather and publicize their remarks. If a customer has experimented with a prototype of your new product and finds it promising, ask that person for a written set of comments. But don't overdo it.

By establishing your trustworthiness *and* expertise, you will build the credibility you need to get your audience's attention and agreement. But to take the next step in the process, you also need to understand your audience and know how it makes decisions.

Understanding Your Audience

No matter how credible people find you and your ideas, you must understand your audience. Specifically, you must do the following:

- Identify decision makers, key stakeholders, and the network of influence within your audience. Which of these people are supportive, in opposition, or neutral? What are their interests, and how do they view their alternatives?

- Analyze your audience's likely receptivity.

- Determine how the people you aim to persuade will make the decisions you hope to influence.

Identify Centers of Influence

In some persuasion situations, you'll present your proposal to one person; in others you will make a presentation to several people, perhaps individually or in a single group session. In either case, you must understand that the opinions of some people are more important than those of others. In most cases, your true audience will usually consist of a subset of people:

- Decision makers

- Key stakeholders

- Influencers

Decision makers are the individuals who can approve or reject your idea. Many persuasion situations involve several decision makers. For example, if you want to hire an additional employee for your unit and you're lobbying your boss for the funds, she may not be the only person you need to persuade. Perhaps your boss's boss may have the final say on new hires. Ultimately, your persuasion efforts must deal with the concerns of decision makers, even though the way to do this may be indirect.

Stakeholders are the individuals directly affected by the acceptance of your proposal. For example, the purchasing manager for an automobile manufacturer is a stakeholder in decisions made by the company's vehicle interior designers. If those designers select a new material for the passenger seats, the purchasing manager will be affected; he will have to locate and negotiate with a suitable supplier.

To identify key stakeholders, think of all the individuals who will be most affected by acceptance of your proposal. In most cases, these will include not only the person to whom you're presenting your proposal but also peers, direct reports, customers, superiors, and board members.

Influencers are individuals who participate indirectly in the decision-making process. They provide advice and information to key stakeholders and decision makers. For example, if you're trying to persuade a marketing manager to launch a new Web campaign, she may turn to the head of information technology for advice on the matter. In this sense, the IT person has influence over the decision.

We commonly refer to some people as *centers of influence* or *opinion leaders* because of their power to influence others around them. These individuals are important to the persuader in that they can influence decision makers even though they have no formal decision-making role. For example, within the Republican world of U.S. politics, William Kristol, editor of the *Weekly Standard,* is an important center of influence—specifically, thought leadership— owing to his frequent columns, media appearances, and access to top party leaders. Among the opposing Democrats, Massachusetts Senator Edward Kennedy plays a similar role. In his position as the party's tribal elder and cloaked in the mantle of the Kennedy legacy, the senator has substantial influence over the policies and positions of fellow Democrats.

Harvard professor Michael Watkins refers to *influence networks* and suggests that persuaders map them out to better understand the complex relationships of influence between members of an organization.[3] Figure 5-1 is an influence map for a four-person team. The degree of influence between individuals is represented there by the style of the arrows that connect them. Thus, Carmen has substantial influence over both Paul and Sonya, but these individuals, judging by the style of their arrows, have less influence over Carmen.

An influence map can help you understand where to apply persuasion in a group setting. Again in this example, if you were trying to persuade Ernest about some matter, you would apply indirect influence through Sonya, and possibly through Carmen because she has influence over Sonya.

Think for a moment about your workplace situation, including your superiors, peers, and subordinates. Sketch out an influence map like the one shown in figure 5-1. Now think about your current efforts to persuade—about obtaining new equipment, a new full-time position, or whatever goal you have in mind. Is your persuasion campaign targeted at the right people? Have you concentrated entirely on the final decision makers while overlooking individuals who might influence them in your favor?

FIGURE 5-1

Influence Map

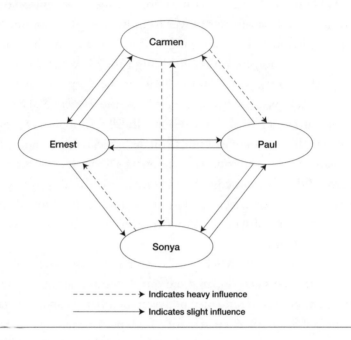

Indicates heavy influence

Indicates slight influence

Note: Appendix B contains tools that can help you be more effective in persuasion situations. You can freely access these tools at the *Harvard Business Essentials* Web site: www.elearning.hbsp.org/businesstools.

Now that you understand the roles of decision makers, stakeholders, and influencers, consider the following case, which brings them all together:

> *Sharon is a sales representative for a college textbook publisher. Her job is to persuade professors to adopt her company's books as required class-room reading. In most cases, the decision process is clear: The professor who teaches a particular course selects the book. In some cases, however, decisions are made by a committee. This is what Sharon discovered*

when she tried to sell her book, Principles of Management, *at XYZ University.*

There are eleven faculty members in the management department of XYZ, and five of them are scheduled to teach sections of Management 101 in the coming fall semester. These five have formed a committee to review the current crop of textbooks and select one for use in all sections of the course. "We want to select a text that will do the job and that every one of us can live with," said one committee member.

At first, Sharon thought that her job would be straightforward: speak with each member of the committee and try to persuade that person to favor her textbook. But as Sharon has learned more about the situation, she has recognized that other factors are at work:

- *There is an evaluation process. Each of the five professors has agreed to evaluate each of the competing books in terms of one or two key topics and then report to the others.*

- *The youngest committee member generally defers to Prof. Viejo, the most senior member of the group, because Viejo has the most experience with undergraduate students.*

- *Another member, Prof. Trimble, has coauthored two journal articles with the author of one of the books under consideration—a direct competitor to Sharon's book. Will that association affect his vote?*

- *Prof. Hardworth, the department chairman, is not a committee member, but he is a clear stakeholder and is leaning hard on the members to select a text that will give students a solid grounding in organization behavior, a course that many of them will take from him in future semesters. "I want them to come out of Management 101 well prepared to take my course," he has told Sharon.*

Sharon is faced with a complex situation. Many currents of influence are at work. Each of the participants—and unofficial participant Hardworth—will have an opinion and will try to persuade the others to buy in to it. Trimble's might be swayed by his professional connection to one particular book. And Viejo might be expected to influence the opinion of the committee's youngest member. Sharon has a challenging job ahead of her.

Sharon's situation is probably similar to ones you've faced in your work—situations with a particular decision-making process, various stakeholders, and cross-currents of influence. How would you handle this one?

Analyze Audience Receptivity

After you've identified all the individuals who make up your true audience, it's time to analyze them. Audiences differ in what they know about your proposal or idea, how interested they are in what you have to say, and how strongly they support your views—all of which influence their receptivity. To analyze audience receptivity, do the following:

- **Monitor reactions.** Look for signs of openness or resistance in e-mails and other formal or informal communications from your intended listeners. During meetings, observe how your listeners voice their concerns or express their opinions about topics related to your idea.

- **Assess body language.** Notice your listeners' tone of voice and body language during casual hallway conversations and other brief, informal exchanges. Does your intended audience seem interested in your ideas? Distracted by other concerns? Skeptical?

- **Talk with knowledgeable people.** Identify individuals who understand your audience's moods and expectations regarding important upcoming company developments. Ask these individuals for their thoughts about the likely receptivity to your idea. Ask what they and the key decision makers and stakeholders care about most, as well as what benefits they see in your idea.

Assess Categories of Receptivity

Audiences generally fall into one of five categories of receptivity: hostile, neutral, uninterested, uniformed, and supportive.

Hostile people disagree with you and may actively block you. To handle them, follow these recommendations:

- Use humor or a story to warm them up to you.

- Focus on areas of agreement.

- Demonstrate your expertise, and cite experts.

- Support statements with solid evidence.

- Stress that you're looking for a win-win outcome.

- Identify benefits that they would value.

It isn't always possible to win over people who start out in a hostile position. But you may be able to move them to a position of neutrality, the next best position for you. Once they become neutral, they will not be working against you.

Neutral people understand your position. They don't favor it, but they are not actively opposed. Your goal is to tilt these neutral people in your favor. In some cases, all that's needed is some convincing or some charming.

- Spell out your proposition's benefits to these listeners.

- Keep it simple. Present only three clear, compelling points, backed by expert evidence, data, and concrete examples.

- Use stories, personal experiences, and anecdotes to appeal to their emotions.

- Point out the downside of *not* accepting your proposal.

- Discuss the alternatives that others might raise.

Uninterested people are informed about your subject but don't care about it. Like neutral listeners, uninterested listeners are not actively opposed to your position, but their lack of interest can be a barrier to your success if a majority is required to win. Again, you must convert them to a position of positively supporting your idea. In many cases, the most powerful antidote to a lack of interest is to appeal to their self-interest. If you can demonstrate that your idea will improve their situations, they may move out of the uninterested camp into yours.

Uninformed people lack the information needed to become convinced and active supporters. In these cases, follow these steps:

- Establish your credibility by showcasing your experience or qualifications.

- Keep your presentation simple and straightforward; don't confuse them with complex evaluations.

- Create an emotional link by sharing personal anecdotes.

Supportive people already agree with you. Your goal is to keep them on your side and make them active agents of influence on your behalf:

- Recharge their enthusiasm with vivid testimonials, and remind them of the benefits at stake.

- Help them anticipate and refute possible arguments from opponents.

- Hand out a detailed action plan with clear deadlines.

Determine Decision-Making Styles

To further boost your odds of persuading those who have the power to accept or reject your proposal, tailor your arguments to fit their decision-making style. People have distinct styles of decision making. In this section we list four styles along with their characteristics and corresponding persuasion strategies.

Here are the decision-making styles and persuasion strategies you can use:

- **The thinker.** A thinker is a cerebral, logical, risk-averse person who needs lots of detail before making a decision. Strategy: Provide as much supporting data as possible to reduce risk. Persuade by using a fact-based approach.

- **The skeptic.** A skeptic will challenge every one of your points but in the end will make a decision based on emotions. Strategy: Establish as much credibility as possible. Invite the skeptic to challenge and play along with the game.

- **The follower.** This person takes his cues from the politically powerful. His thinking will converge with the majority. Strategy: Emphasize references and testimonials. Followers are very interested in how others have dealt with your issue. Understand whom they follow or defer to; if you can get the support of those leaders, the followers will fall in line.

- **The controller.** A controller is unemotional and analytical in making decisions, highly wedded to her own ideas and less open to others. Strategy: Ensure that your argument is sound and well structured. Emphasize outcomes of value to this person.

How can you know which style your decision makers possess? In many cases you can observe a person's decision style in meetings and other workplace interactions. One of the best career moves you can make is to understand how all the people in your immediate workplace make decisions. Once you understand this, you'll enhance your ability to persuade them.

Don't Forget About Politics

We'd all like to believe that a convincing argument will bring people around to our views, but the fact is that good arguments alone are insufficient. That is because politics plays a role in many organization decisions. Every company, division, and operating unit—like every state and city—has its share of political blocs that generally act in concert and in opposition to other blocs.

For example, if Al is in favor of a project, then his political allies, Sandra and Janis, will automatically take his side. Meanwhile, members of an opposing bloc are likely to automatically oppose the project because of their antipathy toward Al. Logical argument will take you only so far in an environment that is this highly charged with politics. The best you can do is to try to understand where politics comes into play, know what motivates people, and understand how people are aligned.

You've now identified key stakeholders, decision makers, and influencers; analyzed your audience; and identified your decision makers' preferred styles. Now you're ready to take the next step: building a case that will capture your listeners' minds—if not their hearts.

Building a Case

Here is every persuader's dream. William has just wrapped up a meeting with three executive decision makers. The first executive initially had been uninterested in William's proposal. The second had come to the meeting with a hostile attitude, and the third had an open mind. But by the end of the meeting, when they had to make the decision, the three looked at each other, shrugged their shoulders, and collectively said, "We cannot argue with you about this proposal, William. It seems perfectly sensible. Let's do it."

This type of ideal outcome is hard to find because a "perfectly sensible" case in favor of anything is difficult to create in a complex world of uncertainty and competing alternatives and interests. Even when a proposal's logic is unassailable, some decision makers will find reasons to resist it. "This would require too large a change for our people." Or "We have other alternatives." Or the objection that no one will admit to: "Your proposal would upset the status quo, from which I benefit immensely even though I'm a total drone." Other objections may have no plausible explanation other than what Mark Twain once referred to as "the cussedness of the human race."

Still, despite natural human resistance, building a rock-solid case remains the basis of effective persuasion. In most cases, a rock-solid case has these characteristics:

- It is logical and consistent with facts and experience.

- It favorably addresses the interests of the parties you hope to persuade.

- It eliminates or neutralizes competing alternatives.

- It recognizes and deals with the politics of the situation.

- It comes with endorsements from objective and authoritative third parties.

When you make a case for something, is it this rock solid? If it isn't, use the preceding bullet points as a checklist for making it so.

Summing Up

- Persuasion is a process that enables a person or group to change or reinforce others' attitudes, opinions, or behaviors. It is essential for success in all relationships—personal and business alike.

- For managers, persuasion has become more necessary as the command-and-control nature of business gives way to employee participation, teams, and joint ventures.

- Persuasion has four elements: credibility, an understanding of the audience, a solid argument, and effective communication.

- Credibility is trust plus expertise. If you want to increase your credibility, increase the level of trust people have in you, your expertise, or both.

- People will perceive you as having expertise if you exercise sound judgment and demonstrate a history of successes.

- When you analyze the audience you hope to persuade, identify the decision makers and centers of influence, determine their likely receptivity, and learn how they make decisions.

- Learn the characteristics of a rock-solid case and use them whenever you aim to persuade.

6

Persuasion II

Winning Minds and Hearts

Key Topics Covered in This Chapter

- *Four approaches to appealing to the logic of your audience*

- *The role of emotions in decision making*

- *How language, vivid descriptions, metaphors, analogies, and stories can help your idea resonate with an audience*

- *The use of persuasion triggers*

YOU'VE PREPARED A logical and rock-solid case that should persuade any fair-minded person. But logic and reason are not everything. Emotions, perceptions, and predispositions also play major roles in how people make business decisions. To persuade others, you thus need to address your listeners' minds *and* their hearts. This chapter focuses on strategies for winning both.[1]

Start with the Head

You can appeal to your listeners' reasoning power in several ways:

- The way you structure your presentation

- The evidence you provide to back up your proposal

- The benefits you emphasize

- The words you use

Begin with the Right Structure

How do you decide what to say first, second, and so on in trying to win people to your point of view? Sometimes your assessment of your audience's receptivity will influence the structure you select. At other times, the subject matter will suggest the appropriate structure.

And you might decide to use one structure to present your case to one audience (for example, a receptive audience) and another to present the same case to another audience (such as a skeptical audience). Consider the following examples of structures:

- **Problem–solution.** Describe a pressing problem, and then solve it by presenting a convincing solution. Use this structure with an uninterested audience or one that's uninformed about the problem.

- **Present both sides and a refutation.** To win over neutral or hostile audiences, argue both sides. First present your opponents' side, thereby showing that you accept the validity of their position and increasing their receptivity. Then refute their case point by point by challenging their evidence and disproving their arguments.

- **Cause and effect.** Discuss the causes underlying a problem, and then show how your idea will eliminate those causes and eliminate the problem. Alternatively, emphasize the undesirable effects of a problem and explain how your proposal will mitigate them. Use this structure for mixed audiences—that is, audiences that contain people who are, variously, receptive, hostile, neutral, supportive, and so forth.

- **Motivational sequence.** Capture your audience's attention with a startling statistic, an anecdote, or a humorous story—and then identify a pressing need. Explain how your proposal will satisfy that need, and help listeners visualize the bright future in store if they adopt your proposal. Finally, tell your audience what actions you want them to take. Use this structure for supportive audiences.

How you begin and end your presentation are especially critical. Capture your audience's attention in the very beginning with a dynamic opening. Conclude with a call for action in which you clearly indicate what you want from your listeners.

Provide Compelling Evidence

The evidence you provide to support your proposal—testimonials, examples, statistics, and graphical evidence—can further strengthen your persuasiveness.

Testimonials enhance persuasiveness when they come from sources your audience considers expert and credible. For example, if you're advocating the adoption of a new technology, provide quotations from respected companies similar to yours that have adopted the technology with excellent results. "Adopting CustomerLinx software helped us cut our service response time in half. Our customers are now a lot happier, and so are the shareholders."—Frank Quisling, VP of Customer Service, Rotary Products, Inc.

Examples further capture people's attention by turning generalizations and abstractions into concrete proof. To illustrate, cite examples of what a proposed new technology can accomplish: "Each of our customers has reported a reduction in customer response time of at least 35 percent within one month of installing and training people on CustomerLinx software."

Statistics are especially effective if you make them understandable and memorable. How? One way is to personalize cold, lifeless numbers: "Four out of ten people in this room exaggerate their expenses." Cite eye-popping comparisons: "Our main competitor is currently generating twice as many sales dollars per employee as we do. Can you imagine what our profit-sharing bonuses would look like if we doubled our sales per employee?"

Graphical materials, such as slides, flipcharts, videotapes, and product samples, can further boost your success at imparting evidence and capturing people's attention. That's because visual information sticks with people. In fact, three-quarters of what people learn is acquired visually. But don't get carried away. Choose a medium that's appropriate to your message. If you employ a Power-Point presentation, convey one concept per slide. Keep it simple and clear. When creating charts and tables, first determine the main trends or patterns you want to emphasize, and then take care not to distort or misrepresent information.

When carefully selected and compellingly presented, evidence in all its forms can win over your listeners through reason.

Spotlight the Benefits Your Listeners Value

The features of your idea—such as how a new software program you're advocating works—may interest some listeners. But its *benefits*—how the idea will make their lives or work easier or more productive—will more strongly attract their attention. People who fail to answer their listeners' question "What's in it for me?" stand little chance of winning their minds. To understand this firsthand, consider table 6-1, which lists a computer's features and benefits. Which column do you find most appealing?

Each benefit may appeal to listeners on one of two primary levels of motivation: the desire for gain and the fear of loss.

- A benefit may enable listeners to gain something they don't currently have—for example, money, time, popularity, possessions, or a good reputation.

- A benefit may enable listeners to avoid losing something they currently have and value. Before the days of credit cards and automatic teller machines, American Express ran television ads showing a family vacation ruined when the hapless father lost his wallet. The message was clear: Don't let this happen to you; carry our traveler's checks.

TABLE 6-1

Features Versus Benefits

Features	Benefits
• The latest microprocessor	• Lets you work faster and use the latest applications
• A 40-gigabit hard drive	• Enables you to store more data and update it faster
• A flat-screen monitor	• Makes it easier to view more, while taking up much less desk space than a traditional monitor

Source: Harvard ManageMentor® on Persuasion, adapted with permission.

Research shows that the fear of loss is actually a more powerful motivator than the prospect of gain. For example, the fear of losing money you already have is a more powerful motivator than gaining money you don't have! So think about which benefits your audience values most. Then develop a unique value proposition for your proposal by asking these questions:

- What benefits does my proposal provide? What will my audience gain? What will they avoid losing?

- What evidence shows that these benefits are real? Are there compelling and credible testimonials, examples, statistics, and graphical representations available to support this?

- What makes my proposal unique? What's different and unusual about my idea? Why should my audience accept my proposal and not others?

By spotlighting the unique advantages of your proposition, you will convince listeners that your idea merits serious consideration.

Note: How well do you understand the people you are trying to persuade? Do you know who the decision makers are? Do you know what constitutes value in their minds? If you need help on this matter, make use of appendix B, which contains tools that can help you understand your audience. A copy of these tools can be downloaded without charge from the *Harvard Business Essentials* Web site: www.elearning.hbsp.org/businesstools.

Select the Right Words

When persuasion is your aim, never underestimate the power of well-chosen words. The words you select can determine whether your listeners consider or dismiss your proposal. Your words should be affirmative, assertive, and responsible, and they should foster collaboration and engender trust. Table 6-2 provides examples of good and bad word selection.

Tips for Defining Your Unique Value Proposition

1. **Brainstorm the benefits.** Think about all the possible benefits of your proposition. What would your audience members gain, and what would they avoid losing, by accepting your proposition?

2. **Prioritize the benefits based on audience interests.** Of the benefits you've identified, which do you think your audience values most? Prioritize audience members' interests based on your understanding of their current problems, concerns, and values.

3. **Gather evidence showing that the high–priority benefits are real.** Collect compelling testimonials from credible sources showing that the benefits that matter most to the members of your audience are within their reach if they accept your proposition. In addition, gather examples, statistics, and graphical representations that speak to the benefits of your proposition.

4. **Play up what makes your proposal unique.** Compare your idea against potential alternative propositions. What's different, unusual, and superior about your idea? Why should your audience accept your proposal and not others? Be ready to explain in succinct, compelling terms what makes your proposal better than others.

Whenever possible—and only when appropriate to your audience—sprinkle attention-grabbing words, such as *easy, free, guaranteed, proven,* and *results,* throughout your persuasion communications. Emphasize key points with words such as *important, imperative, critical,* and *essential* without overdoing it. Most of these words are borrowed from sales and, despite their heavy use, are remarkably effective.

TABLE 6-2

Word Selection Matters

Type of Words Selected	Example of What to Say	Example of What Not to Say
Affirmative language communicates precisely what you expect to happen.	"*When* you finish that report, we'll celebrate by going out for a pizza."	"*If* you finish that report, we'll celebrate by going out for a pizza."
Assertive speech presents your arguments with confidence.	"Our project *needs* additional funding."	"I would *guess* that our project could use additional funding."
Accept responsibility for your circumstances.	"*I'll* have the person who is responsible phone you."	"I *can't* help you."
Win-win language fosters cooperation.	"That's a new approach. *Let's talk it through* to see where we end up."	"Maybe you should run some numbers, because *I don't see that working.*"
Phrasing can make people trust your integrity.	"*This is a much better deal* for you than the previous one."	"*To be perfectly honest,* I think this deal is perfect for you."

Source: Harvard ManageMentor® on Persuasion, adapted with permission.

By structuring your presentation effectively, providing the best evidence, spotlighting your proposal's benefits, and selecting the right words, you boost your chances of winning your listeners' minds. Now let's see how to capture their hearts.

Don't Forget Your Audience's Heart

The most logical argument won't persuade people unless you've also connected with them on an emotional level. In fact, emotions play a more powerful role in human decision making than facts, numbers, and a rational assessment of a proposal's benefits. Why? There are several reasons:

- Emotion-evoking presentations—such as gripping stories—are more interesting and memorable than statistics and facts.

- Emotion tends to prompt behavioral changes more quickly than do logical appeals.

- Responding emotionally requires less effort than logically weighing the pros and cons of a presentation.

- Emotion-arousing arguments distract people from the speaker's intention to persuade.

In the most successful persuasive situations, people *first* accept the presenter's proposal unconsciously, based on their emotional response. Then they justify their decision based on a logical assessment of the facts, as in this example:

> *Ricardo wanted a new car. But not just any car. He wanted a BMW. "What a great-looking car," he told himself as he stood next to the 2001 X5 model he had spotted on the dealer's used-car lot. He admired the sleek lines of its burgundy exterior and the black leather seats. And he was very pleased when the salesman handed him the keys, saying, "Take it for a ride—then talk to me."*
>
> *To Ricardo, the BMW looked great, smelled new, and drove like the finely tuned machine it was. "Oh, man," he muttered as he catapulted onto the expressway and put the car through its paces. "You can really feel the power and agility."*
>
> *Half an hour later Ricardo was in the salesman's office asking technical questions about the car. What parts, if any, were still covered by the original warranty? Did the dealer have the original owner's maintenance log book? What about a trade-in agreement for his current vehicle, a 1996 Toyota? The salesman answered each of his questions and provided still more technical information about the car.*

Ricardo took it all in and even made some notes, but he really wasn't paying attention. He had made up his mind about this car out on the expressway as he moved up through the gears. Later that day, in explaining his purchase decision to his father, Ricardo cited the car's technical merits and the terrific deal he had negotiated. And he believed his own story.

Yes, emotions truly matter. The language you choose and the way you compose your argument exert a major impact on listeners' emotions. So when you present your ideas, use vivid descriptions, metaphors, analogies, and stories that resonate with your listeners.

Note: One warning about emotions. Some audiences want the facts and will react negatively to any presentation that omits them in favor of emotional appeals. Consider the predicament your CEO and CFO would be in if they made a presentation to a group of Wall Street securities analysts and skipped the details of sales and earnings projections. If all they did was give a rosy description of how the company's products were changing people's lives for the better, most of the analysts would get up and leave the room.

Vivid Descriptions

Words that paint evocative images in people's minds deeply tap in to listeners' emotions. For example, let's suppose that you want to persuade your boss to allow some employees to work from their home offices several days each week. You anticipate that the boss will worry that this arrangement may reduce worker productivity and result in loss of control: "How would I know if they are working and not watching *Seinfeld* reruns?" To persuade him otherwise, you should vividly describe those employees working diligently from their home offices, free from the many distractions that permeate the office on a typical workday. You contrast that picture with one of employees being interrupted by frequent meetings and by well-meaning coworkers who stop by to chat. "How many of your meetings are nothing but time wasters?" you ask the boss. "Most of them," he replies.

As you paint these images in your boss's mind, he begins experiencing two emotions: a desire for a more focused, industrious staff, and an aversion to the disruptive reality you've described. To seal the deal, you recognize his concern about loss of control. "In the end, it's results that count, isn't it?" you ask. "If we give each home office worker clear goals with measurable deliverables, we'll know every week and every month who is doing the job and who isn't." With that assurance, the boss agrees to a pilot program of home-based work for a handful of employees.

Metaphors

A *metaphor* is an imaginative way of describing something as something else—for example, "Time is money." *Organizing metaphors* are overarching worldviews that shape a person's everyday actions; for example, "Business is war." People reveal their organizing metaphors through the language they use. For example, a manager who sees business as war might say things like, "We can't concede ground," "We're being outflanked," or "We have to defend market share."

In some cases, persuasion requires changing a person's organizing metaphor. You can do this by replacing the existing metaphor with one that is more in line with what you aim to achieve; for example, you might attempt to replace "business as war" with "business is a partnership." This metaphor focuses a business's efforts on building win-win relationships with key stakeholders rather than on crushing its competitors. You can achieve the same end by highlighting the weaknesses of your audience's worldview using their metaphor. For example, "By focusing on competitors instead of customer support, we've allowed our customer-satisfaction levels to fall."

Yet another approach to altering the organizing metaphor is through examples of other companies that have achieved success using your replacement metaphor, as in, "XYZ's sales have increased 18 percent since the company directed account managers to collaborate with the sales team."

Replacing someone's organizing metaphor is never easy; people cling tightly to their worldview. But by providing powerful evidence of the flaws in an existing metaphor and the veracity of the new one, you can persuade others to consider a different outlook.

Analogies

Analogies—comparisons that include the words *like* or *as*—enable you to relate a new idea to one that's already familiar to your audience. Analogies help people understand and therefore accept a new idea. Analogies also engender feelings of familiarity, which many people find reassuring. Consider this example:

> *Those of you who worked here at Gizmo Products in the 1980s surely remember the wrenching changes we had to make in abandoning our traditional hydraulic steering technology—a dying art—in favor of electronic steering systems. We had to give up decades of accumulated know-how and learn new, often unfamiliar, skills. Some people were unable to make the transition. Fortunately, the company made it through that transition and went on to become a leader in electronic steering. Today we face yet another transition that, like the previous one, will be just as difficult and every bit as critical to our future survival and success.*

Incongruous analogies and those that use humor are all the more memorable. For example, when Benjamin Franklin once said, "Fish and visitors start to smell in three days," he delivered a vivid message of why people tire of visitors who outstay their welcome.

Stories

Stories also help make presentations come alive and drive messages home. They can accomplish the following:

- Grab listeners' attention with riveting plots and characters that audiences can relate to

- Simplify complex ideas and make them concrete

- Evoke powerful emotions among listeners
- Stay in your audience's mind long after the facts and complex details have been forgotten

As an example of successful storytelling, consider a product design manager who wants his team to generate more and better design ideas. His company is located in a region where many people have strong ties to the local community but where the economy is threatened by larger changes in the national economy. The manager evokes intense emotions in his team by telling the story of how competition from a major discount store destroyed businesses in his own hometown. He describes family businesses that have closed, childhood friends who had to move away in search of work, office buildings now vacant, and a crop of "for sale" signs in what were once vibrant neighborhoods.

No one in the audience has been to that town, but all those in the room can picture it, empathize with the plight of its residents, and imagine how their own town could suffer a similar fate if businesses like theirs failed to prosper.

The manager concludes his story by challenging his team to "fight back" by coming up with ideas for "made here at home" products. His team is charged up by the presentation and responds with a number of practical and innovative design ideas that tap local strengths and talents.

Clearly, the language and imagery of stories can help you connect with your audience's emotions and win their hearts. But no matter how skillfully you use them to appeal to listeners' reason and emotions, you'll likely encounter at least some resistance to your proposals. How to deal with resistance is our next topic.

Overcoming Resistance

Even the most carefully thought-out proposal can meet with resistance. Resistance may have several sources. One person may be committed to a position that diametrically opposes yours. Another may disagree with your idea on technical grounds. Yet another may resist for philosophical reasons—for example, while you are advocating for outsourcing some tasks, this person believes that companies should outsource as few as possible.

How do you move a resister to your point of view? The key lies in understanding the resister's position and then presenting the benefits of your idea in terms the resister values. The following guidelines can help.

Identify Resisters' Interests

Each of us has had unique experiences. These experiences have shaped our views of the world and have influenced how we respond to the ideas of others. If you encounter resistance after presenting a proposal, avoid the temptation to keep pressing your case. Instead, think about what may be driving a resister to disagree with you. Adapt your response accordingly.

For example, suppose you are seeking funding to study the merits of entering a new market. The head of research and development (R&D) opposes your plan. She is concerned that entering a new market would channel company resources away from a project she wants to pursue. In her mind, this is a zero-sum game—one in which any gain by you will be a loss for her. In this case, you might want to address her fears by demonstrating that you and she are not in a zero-sum game. You might argue that entering a promising new market will generate more revenues for the company, which in turn will fund a broad range of new projects for the R&D group.

Understand Resisters' Emotions

Most resistance springs from two emotions: distrust and fear.

- **Distrust.** Your audience doesn't like you or what you represent. For example, perhaps the R&D manager just described views marketers as flaky and unempirical. In this case, the marketer should demonstrate a type of seriousness, attention to detail, and reliance on data and evidence that the R&D manager admires in others. At bottom, you must answer the question, "What are the personal characteristics that engender trust on the part of this person?"

- **Fear.** Your audience doesn't like your idea because of potential adverse consequences for them. For example, listeners may worry that your proposed restructuring will cost them their jobs. Allay those fears by addressing them directly.

  The proposed restructuring will affect many positions. There's no doubt about it. But none of you will lose your job as a result. Some jobs will disappear, but others will be created. There will be more than enough work for everyone in this division. Our plan provides for the skill training that some people will need to take on new responsibilities.

When you understand the emotions driving resistance, you will be in a better position to address your listeners' fears and distrust.

Build Trust

One way to improve relationships is to build trust. You can build trust by listening carefully to resisters' concerns. By listening, you demonstrate that you understand and value them as individuals and care about their concerns. When people feel that they've been heard and that their ideas are valued, they will become more open to considering your ideas. You can use the following techniques to demonstrate that you've heard what's on their minds.

- **Paraphrase.** Mirror the resister's points—for example, "So you're saying that you think I'm just advancing the party line." Paraphrasing prompts your listener to respond with comments such as, "Well, yes—I do." By getting the person to agree with you—even in this small way—you establish common ground, and that enables the individual to become more receptive to your ideas.

- **Clarify the issues.** Identify the resister's primary concerns—for example, "So what I hear you saying is that you have two main concerns. The first one you mentioned is probably the most important, right?" Again, you've established a level of understanding and agreement. You've also shown that you're capable of sorting out the vital issues.

Be Consistent in Verbal and Nonverbal Messages

Body language and tone of voice send a message. Make sure that these communication cues are compatible with the content of your spoken message. If they aren't, your resisters may view you as not credible or as conflicted about your position, and that can further stiffen their resistance and distrust. For example, to telegraph confidence in your position, check that your posture is upright, your hand gestures assertive, your gaze direct, and your voice loud enough to be heard—but not so loud as to intimidate or annoy your listeners. Many successful persuaders rehearse nonverbal behaviors just as much as their spoken presentations.

Effective persuaders also recognize when they are becoming overly emotional or angry—two behaviors that are inappropriate and counterproductive in many persuasion situations. In most cases an emotional or angry attitude on your part will provoke the same among the people you hope to convince, defeating your case. If this happens to you, recover by openly acknowledging and apologizing for such behaviors. Having the courage to publicly admit a mistake in this way can help establish trust and credibility.

Present Resisters' Viewpoints Before Presenting Your Own

If you suspect that you'll encounter resistance, prepare a two-sided argument: theirs and yours. During your presentation, acknowledge your resisters' arguments *first*. Doing so will disarm them by removing their opportunity to oppose you. Deprived of this opportunity, they'll be more open to discussion and will participate in solving the problem at hand.

Next, present your argument. Show clearly how it provides a more powerful solution than does your opponents' argument. When possible, show how you've incorporated their ideas, interests, values, and concerns into your solution.

Persuasion Triggers

People respond to persuasion in two ways: consciously and unconsciously. If someone's in a conscious mode, he might respond thoughtfully to a proposal, weighing its pros and cons and attending carefully to the logic and content of the message. In an ideal world, everyone would make decisions in this way. But in reality, many people don't have the time, information, or motivation to do so. Instead, they switch their decision making to an unconscious mode, and this means that they spend less time processing information. They make decisions based more on instinct than on reason. And they resort to persuasion triggers, or mental shortcuts, to decide how to respond to a proposal.[2] Consider this example:

> *Joe, a manager, must choose between a deal offered by Sue (a supplier's representative) and one offered by Bob. After going through the motions of weighing the advantages and disadvantages of the two, Joe chooses Sue's deal, even though it is inferior to Bob's. The reason? Joe likes Sue because she once did him a favor.*

Researchers have identified six persuasion triggers: contrast, liking, reciprocity, social proof, commitment and consistency, and authority.

Contrast

Judgment, like beauty, is always relative. So when people make decisions, they often look for a benchmark against which to assess the merits of their options. Consider this example:

> *The first candidate you interview for a marketing manager position seems far too expensive when she asks for a starting salary of $90,000. Her request looks much more reasonable when you contrast her against the only other suitable candidate, who wants $110,000.*

To activate the contrast trigger, create an "anchor" for judgments of the person you need to persuade. Many salespeople do this by first showing you the most expensive item in a product line. This makes a mid-priced item seem more affordable.

Liking

There's an old saying that we tend to like people who like us. Liking often emerges when people have something in common. Thus, a persuader sets the groundwork by becoming liked by the audience. We observe this in sales situations all the time. An effective salesperson tries to develop a sense of friendship with the potential customer before attempting to make a sale.

How might you activate the liking trigger? Create bonds with peers, supervisors, and direct reports by discovering common interests—whether it's a shared alma mater, a passion for white-water rafting, or a love of cooking. Demonstrate your liking for others by expressing genuine compliments and making positive statements about their ideas, solutions, abilities, and qualities.

Reciprocity

People generally feel a need to repay favors in kind. This almost instinctive wish to reciprocate exists in all societies. Thus, European explorers of the Americas and the Pacific Islands always brought gifts for the people they encountered, and they received gifts in return. Marketers recognize and make use of this natural urge to reciprocate. For example, fund-raisers have found that when they enclose a small, seemingly insignificant gift in an envelope to potential donors, the volume of donations increases markedly.

To activate the reciprocity trigger, follow this rule: Give before you ask. A small favor such as lending a fellow manager one of your staff members for a few days might be repaid fivefold when you later ask for that manager's support on an important project. In considering what to give, look for solutions that meet other individuals' needs as well as your own.

Take a moment to think about what you could give or freely lend to your coworkers or customers. Some of your time? Unused office space? Free samples? If you give these, you may be pleasantly surprised about what your colleagues give you in return.

Social Proof

Individuals are more likely to follow another person's lead if what he is advocating is popular, standard practice, or part of a trend. For example, during the typical public radio fund-raiser in the United States, the announcer will periodically mention the names of listeners who have just pledged their financial support: "Robert and Elizabeth Harding of Salem, Massachusetts, have just become new members. So has Seth Browning of Lexington. So why don't you call now and join Seth and the Hardings to show your support for this public radio station?" That is social proof.

How do you activate the social proof trigger? Remember the power of association: Make a connection between yourself, your company, or your product and individuals and organizations your audience admires: "Our services are used by 440 of the *Fortune* 500 companies in the United States."

Use peer power to influence horizontally. For example, if you're trying to convince a group of resistant people about the merits of a new project, ask a respected employee in the organization who supports the initiative to speak up for it in a team meeting. You'll stand a better chance of persuading your colleagues with this person's testimony.

Commitment and Consistency

People are more likely to embrace a proposal if they've made a voluntary, public, and written commitment to doing so. For example, 92 percent of residents of an apartment complex who signed a petition supporting a new recreation center later donated money to the cause.

To activate the commitment and consistency trigger, make others' commitments voluntary, public, and documented. Suppose, for example, that you want to persuade an employee to submit reports on time. To inspire this behavior, link the employee's commitment to timely reporting to a formal performance improvement plan that both of you sign.

If getting a commitment is difficult, start small. After you have activated this trigger, you can later turn a small commitment into a large one.

Authority

Many people are trained from childhood to automatically obey the requests of authority figures such as parents, doctors, and police. Authority comes from a combination of position and its associated credentials. For example, your authority as a manager in a drug company will be enhanced if you possess medical as well as business qualifications. This is related to the notion of expertise cited earlier.

Appropriate clothes or other trappings of authority can also increase the chances of successful persuasion. Businesspeople who "power dress" for an important presentation improve the odds that their pitch will be successful.

To activate the authority trigger, make sure that the people you want to persuade are aware of the source of your authority. Wear appropriate clothing, and use other trappings of authority as well.

To get the most persuasive power from the six triggers, use several in combination rather than one at a time.

Summing Up

- To persuade others, you need to address your listeners' logic and emotions.

- Logical appeals can be made through the way a presentation or argument is structured, the use of evidence, the benefits you offer, and the words you use.

- Emotions play a more powerful role in human decision making than facts, numbers, and a rational assessment of a proposal's benefits.

- Vivid descriptions, metaphors, analogies, and stories are among the tools you can use to appeal to the emotional side of an audience.

- To overcome resistance, begin by identifying the interests of the resister.

- Resistance is often motivated by distrust and fear, both of which can be overcome to some extent by an effective persuader.

- Some people resort to persuasion triggers, or mental shortcuts, in responding to persuasive appeals. Six of these triggers were explained here: liking, reciprocity, social proof, commitment and consistency, and authority. Use one or more of these to make your proposal more appealing to the emotional side of your audience.

The Knockout Presentation

A Timeless Tool of Persuasion

Key Topics Covered in This Chapter:

- *Presentation structure—the Greek way*

- *Rhetorical devices*

- *Different learning styles of different listeners*

- *How to aim for the head and the heart*

FORMAL PRESENTATIONS are a powerful way to communicate your message and persuade an audience. Businesspeople use formal presentations to report progress to senior management, to sell company products and services to customers, to encourage adherence to a project goal or schedule, to explain the details of a proposal, to make a pitch for development of a new product line, and so forth. Although some presentations aim to do nothing more than convey information, most hope to influence the audience or persuade its members to accept the presenter's point of view.

Take a minute to think about the presentations you've made or sat through during the past month. Chances are that most aimed to alter the audience's thinking or persuade its members to act in a certain way.

This chapter will help you be more persuasive in your presentations. It begins with a proven presentation structure—one that goes back to the ancient Greeks. The next major section explains several rhetorical devices you can use to give your presentation greater impact. Another section explains the learning styles of the typical audience. If you understand these styles and know how to address them, your presentations will be better received. Finally, the chapter offers practical advice about the use of presentation visuals, one of the most valuable—but often ineptly used—presentation techniques.

Presentations: The Greek Way

In learning how to make a great presentation, take a cue from the people who did it first and did it well—the ancient Greeks.[1] The

Athenian Greeks developed a number of presentation techniques as they began their experiment with democratic government. The art of public speaking emerged from this experiment and the legal system that developed in its wake. Indeed, the five-part Greek outline for a persuasive speech—introduction, narrative, argument, refutation, and conclusion—has never been significantly improved. Some twenty-five centuries later, you can use the Greeks' insights to strengthen your own presentations.

The Introduction

Conventional wisdom is to divide a presentation or speech into three parts: tell the audience what you are going to say, then say it, and then tell them what you just said. The Greeks did not subscribe to this approach. They found it predictable and boring—and countless audiences over the ages have agreed. Audiences quickly figure out what you're up to, and once they do, they listen to one of the three parts of the presentation and ignore the rest.

The Greeks used the introduction to prepare the audience to hear the speech favorably. Here are a few of their strategies.

COMPLIMENT THE AUDIENCE. You can never go wrong complimenting the audience.

It is a pleasure being with a group that has demonstrated, once again, what manufacturing excellence stands for.

TALK ABOUT A PREVIOUS SPEAKER. If your presentation is one of a series, refer to a previous speaker who made a deep impression on the audience.

Jane moved us all with her eloquent appeal to the core values of this company. Now, I'd like to talk to you about a subject I feel as strongly about as Jane feels about company values: the work we are doing in the R&D center.

TALK ABOUT THE EVENT. Draw attention to something that is special or unique about the event. Doing so heightens your listeners' interest and gives them a happy sense that the occasion is an important one. They'll listen more closely as a result.

This morning you will have the distinct privilege of meeting three of the most important innovators in our industry.

TALK ABOUT A MOMENT IN HISTORY. If you can put the time and date of the presentation into historical context, the audience will derive a greater sense of purpose and gravity.

Three years ago, I stood at this same podium and described to you the desperate financial condition of our company. What a difference three years have made.

TALK ABOUT THE PLACE. The hall, the town, the state, or even the country where the presentation takes place is grist for the introductory mill.

This little town—a town that two hundred years ago witnessed our nation's first stirrings toward freedom and the establishment of a new, democratic country—is today the proud site of the new Patriot Shopping Mall.

TALK ABOUT THE POINT OF THE SPEECH. An earlier chapter described framing as a valuable tool of influence. It is your privilege as the presenter to frame the topic and the context for the conversation you will have with the audience.

We're here today to talk about our company's profits over the past six months. Frankly, profitability has been disappointing. What really lies at the heart of the profit issue is customer satisfaction, and I'd like to spend a little time addressing that.

The Narrative

The essence of the narrative is a story. Here you must get to the heart of the matter, whether it involves something you want your listeners to do, or something you want to tell them about. If you don't find yourself phrasing what you have to say in terms of a story, rethink the material. Put the essence of your communication into a story that relates the facts in the way you wish your audience to understand them.

Before I describe the exciting things that are happening in the R&D center today, let me take you back fifteen years and talk about the individual who set the course we are now following: Mark Johnson. Mark had more curiosity and innate inventiveness than any laboratory scientist I've ever met. And he taught all who worked with him to think beyond what customers say they want to the latent needs that customers can't articulate. It is those latent needs that we are addressing with our current development programs.

The Argument

In the argument part of your presentation, you present the proofs, or supporting logic, for your view. This section is probably the most important part of the presentation. Remember that audiences recall very little of what they hear. For this reason, keep your factual evidence to the necessary minimum and your main arguments to three or four at the most. Trying to present more than that will actually weaken your case, because your audience will become exasperated and begin to believe that you are trying to bolster a weak argument with every point you can think of.

It is helpful to provide transitional comments throughout this section to help guide your audience through your arguments.

There are three reasons why expansion of the city's nine-hole golf course would be fiscally unsound. First, the course's reported earnings are substantially overstated—by almost 50 percent. This is a consequence of amateurish profit-and-loss accounting by the Parks Department. Second, there is no adequate water supply. The city is already struggling to meet the water needs of its residents and businesses; an expanded course will divert water resources from their needs. And third, the opening of two new golf courses in the area within the past few years has created an imbalance in supply and demand. Consequently, revenues from an expanded course would be disappointing.

The Refutation

In the fourth section of the Greek speech model, you anticipate objections to your argument. This section is particularly important when the subject is controversial. You must give a real hearing to opposing points of view, even if you intend to subsequently demolish them. Failure to address objections will cause your audience to complain that you never considered opposing points of view. The more explosive the topic, the more important it is to state those points of view and to do so early in the refutation.

You can handle the refutation in two ways:

1. Answer anticipated rebuttals to your own arguments. "People have told me to forget about building product lines around new technologies. 'Business is good,' they say, 'so why change anything?' Business was also good for vacuum tube manufacturers before the era of transistors. But one day those companies woke up and found that technological change had left them behind—and almost every one of them has disappeared. We are confronting a similar possibility today."

2. Take the opportunity to reject your opponents' arguments. Again, this tactic is essential for highly controversial topics. "To those who say that the data storage system I've been advocating will simply cannibalize our current storage system business, I say this: Wouldn't you rather that we did it than have someone else do it to us?"

The Conclusion

The conclusion should not summarize your arguments; rather, it should appeal to the audience for its understanding, its action, and its approval—whatever it is you want the audience to do or think. So don't fall into the trap of telling your audience what you've already said. Summing up is a surefire way to kill any enthusiasm your presentation may have generated. So forget about a summary; instead, tell your audience what it should think or do.

As you leave here today, do so with the confidence that the products you represent are the best on the market, have the strongest service backing in the industry, and are priced to provide the greatest value to customers.

Rhetorical Devices

The ancient Greeks didn't simply develop a five-part structure for making a presentation. They also developed rhetorical devices for connecting with audiences—devices that remain highly effective today. These include parallel structure, triads, antithesis, and rhetorical questions. You can use these in making your presentations more effective and persuasive.

Parallel Structure

Parallel structure uses sentence elements that are alike in both function and construction. Parallel structure is especially useful in presentations because the repetition of language structure helps audiences hear and remember what you have to say. Consider Churchill's speech on Dunkirk to the House of Commons in June 1940:

We shall not flag or fail. We shall go on to the end. We shall fight in France. We shall fight on the seas and oceans. We shall fight with growing confidence and growing strength in the air. We shall defend our island, whatever the cost may be. We shall fight on the beaches. We shall fight on the landing grounds. We shall fight in the fields and in the streets. We shall fight in the hills; we shall never surrender.

You can use similar language structure to good effect in persuading people to accept a course of action: "We will work hard. We will work smart. We will create a better future for the company and for ourselves."

Triads

The Greeks noticed early on that people are attracted to lists of three items. Whether you call it the Rule of Threes or simply a *triad*, a group of three seems to our minds complete and satisfying. No one is quite sure why. The end of Martin Luther King's famous "I Have a Dream" speech illustrates the use of triads. He liked them so much that he gave his audience a double dose:

> *When we let freedom ring, when we let it ring from every village and every hamlet, from every state and every city, we will be able to speed up that day when all of God's children, black men and white men, Jews and Gentiles, Protestants and Catholics, will be able to join hands and sing in the words of the old Negro spiritual, "Free at last! Free at last! Thank God Almighty, we are free at last!"*

You can use triads to good effect in any number of business presentations:

> *Our new reflective window film will reduce your air-conditioning costs, eliminate annoying glare, and protect your furnishings from sun damage.*

Here's another example.

> *The new strategy will work if we do our job as managers. That means articulating our goals, making sure that every employee understands how his or her job fits with the strategy, and aligning rewards with the right behavior at every level.*

Antithesis

In rhetoric, *antithesis* is the placing of a sentence or one of its parts in opposition to another to capture the listener's attention or to evoke a strong response. Consider, for example, the motto of the American state of New Hampshire: Live Free or Die.

Antithesis is rarely used today, even though it is an elegant form of expression and one that people remember vividly. Consider President John F. Kennedy's inaugural address in January 1961. The entire speech was laced with antithesis, but the passage toward the end had particular potency because it spoke directly to the audience:

> *And so, my fellow Americans, ask not what your country can do for you; ask what you can do for your country.*

Because of its dramatic effect, antithesis is less available to the business speaker. Still, you may find opportunities:

> *The choice is ours. We can live with the defender's dilemma, or we can grasp the innovator's advantage.*

Rhetorical Questions

Rhetorical questions are questions asked for the sole purpose of producing an effect. The speaker does not expect the question to be answered—least of all by the audience. Rhetorical questions draw listeners in to the topic by calling for answers, even if those answers are not uttered. Consider Patrick Henry's famous speech of March 1775, only one month before the initial armed clashes of the American revolution:

> *Gentlemen may cry, "Peace! Peace!" but there is no peace. The war is actually begun! The next gale that sweeps from the north will bring to our ears the clash of resounding arms! Our brethren are already in the field! Why stand we here idle? What is it that gentlemen wish? What would they have? Is life so dear, or peace so sweet, as to be purchased at the price of chains and slavery?*

Having posed his rhetorical questions, Henry answered them in the strongest terms:

> *Forbid it, Almighty God! I know not what course others may take, but as for me, give me liberty, or give me death!*

Note the antithesis in Patrick Henry's last sentence.

Tips for Speaking with Confidence

In making a persuasive presentation, it's not only what you say that matters. How you say it will have an impact on your audience. So make the most of these tips:

- **Vary your speaking pace to suit your purpose.** Speaking fast helps you excite and energize your audience, whereas a slow pace creates a mood of anticipation. For most of your presentation, the best pace is to speak slowly enough for listeners to follow but quickly enough to sustain their interest.

- **Use a low pitch to project authority.** Many people interpret a low-pitched voice as authoritative and influential. Similarly, completing a sentence with a downward inflection (a lowering of pitch) communicates confidence and certainty.

- **Control loudness.** Speak loudly enough to be heard but not so loudly as to irritate or offend listeners. To dramatize a moment, try lowering the volume of your voice. Stress important words and phrases with a bit more loudness.

- **Sharpen your articulation.** Clear, crisply articulated words and phrases convey confidence and competence. Such enunciation is also easy to follow.

- **Use pauses for impact.** A correctly timed pause can help you emphasize information and create a desired mood in your audience. It can also alert your audience to a special point. The key is to pause just before the point you want to emphasize—for example, "Our sales increased . . . 25 percent this year." Count "one, two, three" to yourself while pausing, and maintain eye contact with your listeners during the pause.

As a businessperson, you have ample opportunities for posing rhetorical questions and for stating your reply to them. Consider this example:

> *If we continue following the same ineffective strategy, this company can expect the same result: shrinking market share and declining profitability. Do you want to work for a company like that? Are you comfortable with mediocrity? I doubt it. That's why I have offered this plan, and why I'm here today to ask for your support.*

Different Listeners–Different Learning Styles

Another point to remember as you develop and present your ideas is that different audience members are likely to have different primary styles of learning.[2] You may be familiar with the three learning styles, typically referred to as visual, auditory, and kinesthetic. Most people are strong in one of these styles and weaker in the others.

- **Visual learners.** These learners respond best to pictures, graphs, and other visual stimuli. Research shows that 30 to 40 percent of people are visual learners.

- **Auditory learners.** As you may have guessed, these people are more responsive to words and other sounds. An estimated 20 to 30 percent of the population are auditory learners.

- **Kinesthetic learners.** This type of person is most engaged by physical activities: handling a prototype, working at a laboratory bench, or watching a presenter who moves around, mingles with the audience, or uses props. Some 30 to 50 percent of people are kinesthetic learners.

If you want to get the attention of these different types of learners and get them to respond to your message, then your presentation must be couched in their learning modes. Otherwise, you'll lose your audience.

Adaptation to different learning styles is easier said than done, because we can never be certain about the preferred style of a particular audience. Moreover, any audience is bound to contain a mixture of visual, auditory, and kinesthetic learners. The best way to deal with these issues is to provide something for everyone—some blend of visual, auditory, and kinesthetic styles.

To appreciate how the different styles might be employed, consider a typical business presentation. One of your colleagues is reporting the last quarter's results. She stands in front of the group, turns on the overhead projector or her computer, and cues up the first slide. A sea of words and numbers greets your weary eyes. She then launches into reading every word on the screen. You shift in your chair, trying to get comfortable. As slide after slide winks by and your colleague continues to drone on in a flat voice, you gradually sink into a stupor. At the end, you shake yourself awake and exit the meeting room wondering, "What was that about?"

Here's how the three learning styles could be applied to this doleful scene.

Add a dose of visual learning. Like most presenters, your colleague thinks she has appealed to the visual learners by using slides. But most business slides are covered border to border with words, when what visual learners need is pictures—preferably, simple ones. So connect your key concepts visually to angles, circles, squares, and the like. Don't get fancy. It's simply not necessary, and it doesn't promote learning. In addition to pictures, you can use tables and other illustrations for variety—but keep in mind that simpler is usually better.

Cue up your auditory learners. You reach auditory learners through talk—but certain kinds of talk work better than others. Storytelling is one. Parables and anecdotes appeal to auditory learners and are often memorable. In addition, you can employ discussion groups, debates, question-and-answer sessions, and the like—anything that will get you talking in ways more connected to a story than the usual discursive style of business presentation.

Add liveliness through kinesthetic learning. Kinesthetic learners may be the most neglected people at business presentations. Much of what goes on in the business world appeals to the head and not the body, and presentations are rarely exceptions to this dismal rule. The key here is to get your listeners to do something. Get them involved early and often through role-playing, games, working with models, even creating charts and physical representations of what you want them to learn. For example, you can increase your listeners' energy enormously at the opening of a speech simply by having them stand up and shout something appropriate or fun. It's corny, but it works. That's because you have appealed to the kinesthetics in the audience.

If you use all three of these learning modes in a presentation, your audience will pay great attention and remember more.

Note: Visual images containing text and graphics have become a standard feature in formal presentations, so it is imperative that you master them. When used judiciously, visual images can get key points across and make them memorable. Used without thought or discipline, however, these tools can actually confuse or bore the audience, diminishing the impact of an entire presentation. To learn how to make the most of visual aids, see appendix C, "Commonsense Rules for Presentation Visuals."

Aim for the Head *and* the Heart

We have already addressed the subject of audience emotions in chapter 6's discussion of persuasion. It is worth revisiting here in the context of formal presentations.

Our business culture has a decided slant toward the analytical and cerebral. So it's not surprising that many presenters concentrate on the logic of their arguments and quantitative supporting evidence. An emotional component isn't there, or, if it is, it is buried under a mountain of facts and figures. In making a case for the development of a new product, for example, a presenter will inevitably roll out lots of product specifications, pro forma financial statements, and other numerical fireworks. All this information aims for the head.

Many business issues, however, have unstated personal and emotional components. These components may exert substantial power over listeners. Consider a new product-line concept as an example. On the surface, it's all about potential revenues, cost estimates, marketing issues, and good fit with company strategy. Beneath the surface, however, the new product line may affect individual listeners in important ways, including the following:

- **As a threat.** "If that new product line performs as predicted, the importance of my product line will be overshadowed."

- **As an opportunity to benefit personally.** "If this thing works, our annual bonuses will triple. I could help my kids pay off their college loans, or I could retire early."

- **As a change in the workplace.** "If it works as planned, that new product line would make a big difference around here. We wouldn't always be worried about layoffs and budget cuts. People would enjoy coming to work for a change."

A good presentation recognizes these emotion-laden concerns. The presenter speaks to the head *and* the heart. In doing so, he engages listeners at a deeper level. Consequently, after you've presented the intellectual side of your story, shift to its deeper personal meaning for the audience. And use personal pronouns to signal your shift from cold-blooded objectivity:

That concludes our presentation of the revenue and cost estimates for the proposed product line. We have confidence in those estimates and the long-term profits they point to. We believe, too, that this product line has the power to change our company in fundamental ways—and for the better. If you're tired of apologizing for our outdated designs and technology, these new products will restore your pride in what we stand for. If you're tired of being a market follower, these products will make us the market innovator and the company that customers look to for technical leadership.

Did you notice all the personal pronouns in that ending: *we, you, you're, our?* Don't lay it on too thick, but speak to the hearts of your listeners if it's appropriate to the situation and if you want to make a real impression.

Be Prepared to Answer Questions

Questions taken from the audience are a useful way to engage listeners and drive your persuasive points home. The best time for Q&A is at the very end; this allows you to complete your delivery as planned. It's also a good idea to let the audience know at the very beginning that you'll provide time for questions at the end. Doing so has two benefits: It prevents unwanted interruptions, and it ensures that listeners will have heard your entire presentation before they ask questions. Taking questions during the presentation keeps people engaged and gives you feedback about how well they understand your message. But this approach may cause you to lose control of your talk.

Anticipate Likely Questions

Q&A entails risk for the presenter. If she must repeatedly say, "I don't know," "I'm not sure," or "I'll have to get back to you on that," the credibility of the presentation will suffer. That risk can be reduced if the speaker anticipates and develops answers for likely questions as part of the presentation preparation.

You can anticipate likely questions if you take the trouble to understand your audience. Who will attend the presentation? Why are they coming? What are their concerns? How is the presentation likely to strike them? Which of your arguments conflict with what they currently believe? For example, if your presentation concerns the adoption of a new employee dental insurance plan, you'll want to have answers to specific and predictable questions at the ready—unless you cover them in the body of the presentation:

How much will employees have to contribute to the plan each month?

Is there an annual deductible that employees must pay before the plan benefits kick in?

Does the plan cover orthodontia?

Are all family members automatically covered by the plan?

If not, what is the cost of additional coverage?

It's impossible to anticipate and prepare for every question that may come your way. For this reason, you must be prepared to think on your feet and know how to redirect questions. In this respect, you have four tools: feedback, paraphrasing, clarification, and empathy.[3]

Give Feedback

Feedback is a form of two-way communication. A person says something, and you respond, giving your reaction to what was said, as in the following example.

You're a senior manager responsible for developing a new software product that is late to market and far over budget. You've been asked to rally the troops and urge them on. You finish your talk with some stirring words about pioneers and landing on the moon. You hope that your remarks didn't sound too goofy, and then it's time for Q&A. The first question comes from a person in the back of the room.

"Pardon my skepticism, but we've been hearing this same stuff from senior management for months now. We don't need another pep talk. What we really need is more help and a lot less red tape."

This is the question you most feared. You begin to think that your speech has had no impact. You take a deep breath, and respond.

"The fact is that we're committed to getting you more help. We're struggling to hire qualified people. But as you know, qualified soft-

ware developers are very hard to find right now. And we don't want to create more problems by hiring second-best personnel who will make your work more difficult. If you know of any qualified software developers, please get in touch with Human Resources and give the department this information.

"As for red tape, we'd like to think that we eliminated most of it when we set you up in a separate building and organized the project into self-managing teams. Next question?"

On the surface, in this example, you've responded to each of the points raised by the questioner. And yet your response may do little to cure the questioner's negative attitude—an attitude that others may share. You could have done more, as demonstrated next.

Paraphrase the Question

Paraphrasing the question is a technique for mirroring the questioner's points. It indicates that you are listening and interested in what that person has to say. Let's look at how this tool works in the same example.

So what you're saying is that I'm just giving the party line when what you really need is more help and less red tape. Is that right?

The questioner's likely response is yes. Now the hostile questioner is agreeing with you. You can then go on to give your feedback, in the words used in the case study example, but to a more receptive listener. But there are even better ways to respond.

Clarify the Issues

In clarifying the issues, you work a little harder with the questioner's words to identify his real concerns. Let's see how that would happen here.

So what I hear you saying is that you see two key problems: too few people and too much red tape. The first is probably the most important. Is that right?

Again, you've established a level of agreement with the questioner. By clarifying, however, you've gone a step further. You've shown the audience that you're genuinely interested in trying to sort out the vital issues. In this way, you keep better control of the Q&A session.

Demonstrate Empathy

Empathy is the ability to identify with or vicariously experience the thoughts or feelings of others. Anything you can do during a presentation to demonstrate genuine empathy will improve your standing with the audience and will help neutralize any subliminal hostility. As former U.S. President Bill Clinton was fond of stating, "I feel your pain." Members of the audience who sense genuine empathy will think, "She understands our problems" or "She's really one of us. We can trust her." And trust opens the door to persuasion.

The Q&A session is one of the obvious places where you can demonstrate empathy with your audience, as in our software project example.

> *I recognize the hardship that long hours and too few helping hands have caused people on your team. One person told me just last week about how she had to miss her daughter's first soccer game. I have young kids, too, so I know how she must feel. That's why we're sending HR people to every software job fair and doing everything we can to find qualified people who can lighten your load.*

Aim for Continuous Improvement

Like other activities, a presentation is the result of a process that converts inputs (your ideas, information, and arguments) to outputs (what your audience sees and hears). And like other processes, it can be improved.

Process improvement—whether it has to do with making automobiles or making persuasive presentations to the board of directors—is the foundation of quality. The quality movement that swept

Tips for Handling Q&A

The following tips can help you and your listeners get the full benefit from your presentation.

• Make a clear transition to the Q&A session.

• If the audience is large, repeat the question for the audience to hear.

• Maintain control of Q&A by rephrasing the question and giving the answer to the whole group and not only to the questioner.

• If you don't know the answer to a question, direct the person to a source for the answer, or offer to get the answer later.

• If you get a hostile question, find the reasons for the hostility. Acknowledge valid points, and reject those that are not accurate. Then politely move on.

• Don't allow a long-winded questioner to monopolize the Q&A session. Say, "So that other people get a chance to talk, let me stop you there and see if I can answer the question."

through manufacturing in the 1980s and through services in succeeding years has taught us that if we want a higher level of output quality, we should look first to the output itself. Is it up to standard, or are there measurable defects? When defects are found, we must trace them back to their root causes. When these causes are known, we can take corrective action.

Follow this same approach after every presentation. If you take the time to objectively evaluate a presentation after the fact (or after a rehearsal), you will be able to pinpoint the root causes of poor performance. For example, you may find cluttered overheads, weak opening remarks, inept attempts at humor, or something else. When you've identified the problems, do something about them as you prepare for your next presentation. In that way, you'll never make the same mistake twice.

One of the best ways to evaluate your performance and to pinpoint areas for improvement is to videotape and review each presentation or rehearsal. If this is not possible, ask one or more helpful colleagues to note what went well and what went poorly. An after-action review of the tape or the colleagues' notes will put you in touch with the best and worst of your presentation skills. If you work on continuous improvement, your presentations will become increasingly effective—and your standing in the organization will rise.

Summing Up

- The Greek approach to public speaking involves a five-part structure: the introduction, narrative, argument, refutation, and conclusion. You can use the same structure for organizing and delivering business speeches and presentations.

- The introduction prepares the audience to be receptive.

- In the narrative, the speaker tells his or her story.

- In the argument, the speaker presents supporting logic.

- The speaker then uses refutation to anticipate and rebut possible objections to his or her position.

- The conclusion appeals to the audience for acceptance or a particular action.

- The four rhetorical devices used by the Greeks to connect with and convince their listeners are parallel structure, triads, antithesis, and rhetorical questions. These devices are as useful today as they were ages ago.

- The three primary learning styles of listeners are visual, auditory, and kinesthetic. Presenters should adjust their talks to the known learning style of their audiences. When the style is mixed or unknown, the speaker should include something for everyone.

- Don't simply address the intellects of your listeners; speak also to their emotions by making the personal impact of your proposal clear.

- Use a Q&A session to deepen your connection with the audience and to further persuade.

- Apply the principles of continuous process improvement to your presentation. If you do this, you will get better and better—and more persuasive—over time.

The Ethics of Power, Influence, and Persuasion

Points to Honor

Key Topics Covered in This Chapter

- *Two standards to which ethical power must conform*

- *Pressures on the ethics of young managers*

- *The frequent use of manipulation*

- *Five ways to create an ethical culture*

POWER, INFLUENCE, and persuasion have one thing in common with explosives. When used carefully and for well-intentioned purposes, all are capable of good. Most of us know the damage that they can cause when handled carelessly, irresponsibly, or with evil intent.

Power corrupts those who wield it, as the example of every tyrant from Caligula to Pol Pot verifies. Influence can also be malignant. Shakespeare's *Othello* has given us a powerful example in Iago, who uses his influence to manipulate and destroy the people who trust him. And we all know of silver-tongued persuaders who will say anything, promise everything, and eventually deliver nothing; these people will do whatever it takes to get what they want: a sale, a promotion, an election day victory.

These examples, however, should not dissuade us from the legitimate uses of power, influence, and persuasion. Each has an important role to play in business and in everyday life. This chapter addresses the ethical issues associated with their use.

The Ethical Exercise of Power

When historian Lord Acton (1832–1902) warned his students and his readers that "Power tends to corrupt, and absolute power corrupts absolutely," he did so because of his concern for the danger posed to liberty by holders of political power. And there is no shortage of evidence that his concern was well founded. As a scholar of the classics, Acton was familiar with tyrannies among the ancient Greeks and with the history of Rome, in which the virtues and liberties of republicanism were swept away by absolutist emperors. One need only read Suetonius' account *The Twelve Caesars* to appreciate how power can lead to tyranny, and to the debasement of those who hold it.

We have seen in our own time what can happen when one person has inordinate power over others. People around the world were shocked in mid-2004 by news accounts of how some U.S. soldiers had abused and humiliated prisoners held in Iraq's Abu Ghraib jail. How could members of a professional army—people who had grown up in the same types of homes as the rest of us—do these things? Could it be that the prison scandal was merely the fault of a few bad apples?

Apologists cited inadequate training and lack of supervision by superior officers. But these explanations seem inadequate. At the heart of the problem was the unchecked and unaccountable power that the guards had over their prisoners—the same power that Acton warned of more than a century earlier. More to the point, this type of abuse—and even worse torments—has been standard procedure in the same prison during the Saddam Hussein regime, when similar conditions prevailed. As if to demonstrate that the corruptive influence of absolute power has no nationality, we know that American prisoners of previous military conflicts had experienced even worse abuses at the hands of Japanese, North Korean, and North Vietnamese captors.

Oddly, the prisoner abuses exposed in 2004 could have been predicted by a simulated prison experiment conducted at Stanford University in 1971 under the guidance of psychologist Philip Zimbardo. There, in the basement of the university's psychology department building, seemingly normal people became abusive when given power over others.

Reflecting on that experiment in light of the Iraqi situation, Zimbardo identified the situational settings in which things like this occur. "My research and that of my colleagues has catalogued the conditions for stirring the crucible of human nature in negative directions. Some of the necessary ingredients are: diffusion of re-sponsibility, anonymity, dehumanization, peers who model harmful behavior, bystanders who do not intervene, and a setting of power differentials."[1] The last three of these conditions are found in some business organizations.

The Stanford Prison Experiment

The simulated prison situation set up and monitored by Zim-bardo and his colleagues aimed to determine what happens when you put normal people in a situation where they have power over others—in this case, as prison guards. Would they retain their humanity, or become abusive and evil? More specif-ically, the team wanted to observe the psychological effects of becoming a prisoner or prison guard.

A group of mentally well-balanced, intelligent, middle-class male volunteers was randomly divided into two groups: prison-ers and guards. Although both groups understood that they were merely part of a simulation, the line between simulation and prison reality quickly faded. As Zimbardo would write later, "The planned two-week study was terminated after only six days because it was out of control. Good boys chosen for their normalcy were having emotional breakdowns as powerless pris-oners. Other young men chosen for their mental health and positive values eased into the character of sadistic guards inflict-ing suffering on their fellow students without moral compunc-tion. And those 'good guards' who did not personally debase the prisoners failed to confront the worst of their comrades, allow-ing evil to ripen without challenge."[a]

The details of the Stanford prison simulation can be viewed at www.prisonexp.org.

[a] Philip G. Zimbardo, *The Boston Globe*, May 9, 2004. View at <www.boston.com/news/globe/editorial_opinion/oped/articles/2004/05/09/power_turns_good_soldiers_into_bad_apples>.

Yes, power has the capacity to corrupt. But power is necessary to the functioning of organizations and society. How do we get the latter and not the former? The solution is the ethical use of power. Power used ethically conforms to these two standards:

1. It is exercised to benefit the entity from which power is derived and that it is responsible to serve.

2. It conforms to cultural or legal standards of ethical behavior.

The first of these conditions represents the lowest order of the ethical exercise of power. Here, the person wielding power recognizes that he must use that power in the best interests of the organization that invested him with it.

For example, if an executive exercises power in support of a research project that, if successful, will benefit his organization, he is acting in an ethical manner. Thus, former General Electric CEO Jack Welch acted ethically when he used his power to obtain discretionary funds for a struggling R&D project—an unusual step in that his action was outside the review process normally used to allocate resources. The engineers and scientists working on that project were trying to develop an X-ray system based on digital technology. Normally, project funding was conducted through a formal process, but Welch, seeing the great potential of this struggling endeavor and its troubles in getting funding, used his considerable power of position to intervene.[2] His intervention kept the project alive. The project eventually reached the point where it could obtain funding through normal channels, and it went on to great success, producing revenues for GE and its shareholders.

In contrast to the ethical exercise of organizational power, you can probably cite examples of executives and politicians who have used the power vested in their positions for personal gain or for the benefit of their friends and family. Consider this true example:

Homeowners in a medium-sized community found a letter enclosed with their quarterly water and sewer bills. It was written on city stationery and signed by the city's commissioner of public works. The letter advised homeowners of a special form of insurance offered by a private

company—an insurance policy that would pay for the repair and re-
placement of any broken underground water pipes on their property.
Without explicitly recommending that homeowners should buy policies
from this company, it did provide the company's phone number and
urged that homeowners call if they had any interest.

> *Many wondered, "Why are city officials using taxpayer time and*
money to publicize the services of a for-profit, private company?
Shouldn't that company be doing its own advertising—just like every
other business?" Digging into the story, an enterprising news reporter
discovered close ties between the city's mayor and the marketing vice
president of the insurance company. Furthermore, two years earlier the
mayor had encouraged the previous public works commissioner to send
the same letter to homeowners. But that individual refused, saying that
it seemed unethical.

If the mayor had, in fact, used the power vested in him by the community to benefit the insurance executive and his company, then that would have been an unethical use of power.

Our second condition for the ethical exercise of power—that it must conform to cultural or legal standards of ethical behavior—trumps the first. Thus, using power to the advantage of your organization is unethical if it is illegal or if it fails to meet the standards of behavior expected by the community. Consider this example:

> *A salesperson is empowered to represent her company's products to cus-*
tomers with the goal of obtaining orders. If she makes the best case for
those products in a truthful manner, she will be acting ethically. Lying
and other forms of deception would clearly benefit her company—at least
in the short term—but would violate cultural (and perhaps legal) stan-
dards of ethical behavior. She would be exercising her power unethically.

Everyone who works for an organization faces the dilemma inherent in these two aspects of ethical behavior. Here, the cynic's definition of a diplomat comes to mind: "an honest person sent abroad to lie on behalf of his country." People are routinely forced to choose between what is best for the organization and what is right in terms of higher ethical standards. Harvard professor Joseph Badaracco Jr.

found clear evidence of this in a research study based principally on interviews with thirty recent Harvard Business School graduates. Badaracco describes what happened:

> In many cases, young managers received explicit instructions from their middle-manager bosses or felt strong organizational pressure to do things that they believed were sleazy, unethical, or sometimes illegal. Second, corporate ethics programs, codes of conduct, mission statements, hot lines, and the like provided little help. Third, many of the young managers believed that their company's executives were out-of-touch on ethical issues, either because they were too busy or because they sought to avoid responsibility.[3]

Interviewees cited pressures from their powerful bosses that put them in ethical dilemmas. One was told to make up data to support his boss's plan. "Just do it," he was told. Another cited several cases in which whistle-blowers—people who brought unethical or illegal practices to the attention of top management—met with disastrous personal consequences. Still others feared that doing the right thing would cost them their jobs.

The Ethics of Influence and Persuasion

Whether your influence is direct or indirect, influence is most effective when it is based on mutual gain. Ethical practitioners recognize opportunities for mutual gain inherent in any situation. Indeed, this is one hallmark of a master negotiator: the ability to identify and pursue win–win opportunities. These people also consider the long-term implications of everything they do. They know that unethical tactics can destroy in an instant a reputation of trust and credibility built over years. When that goes, their ability to influence goes with it.

Perhaps the greatest violation of the ethical use of influence is manipulation. In their book *Influence Without Authority*, Allan Cohen and David Bradford define *manipulation* as "actions taken to achieve influence that would be rendered less effective if the other party knew one's actual intentions."[4] Here are a few examples of unethical influence:

- Exaggerating your demands in a negotiation, knowing that you can settle for less and still achieve your goals. For example, a labor union representative would be happy to receive a 4 percent pay increase in a new contract but asks for more: "The compensation of our people has been losing purchasing power due to inflation for several years. We need a 7 percent raise just to catch up."

- Concealing your true intentions in order to influence a better outcome for yourself. Consider the example of a manager who is trying to rid herself of a poorly performing subordinate. "I hate to lose you," she lies, "but taking that open position in the logistics department will help you get ahead in the company."

- Deliberately providing false information to gain advantage. "I've heard that David Jones plans to take early retirement this year," the manager lies to an associate he is trying to recruit to his team. "So joining David's project team instead of mine would be a very bad career move for you. Once he's gone, his team will be a ship without a rudder."

Manipulative practices such as these can produce short-term gains at the expense of others; these are win-lose situations. But as Cohen and Bradford point out, the manipulator is eventually found out, and her future ability to influence is compromised, making her ineffective in future dealings. "Fooling some of the people some of the time is not enough for sustained success in today's interdependent organizations," they write. "Those who lie to get their way are almost inevitably found out and then frozen out of the action by peers and bosses who do not trust them . . . A reputation for shady practices, or even for constant self-interest at the expense of others, is corrosive; colleagues and bosses resist the influence attempts of those they don't trust."[5]

The sin of omission—that is, failing to reveal facts that would jeopardize your case—is another tool of manipulation, and one that tempts people who persuade. Consider this example:

> *Jean-Michel, a representative of a stock brokerage firm, is talking with a client on the telephone. The subject is the forthcoming issue of shares of DataTrix, Inc., a fast-growing young software company. Jean-Michel believes that DataTrix has great business potential and that buying its shares at this early stage could result in very high returns. "Who knows?" he tells his client. "This might be the next Microsoft."*
>
> *Jean-Michel also understands that high potential returns go hand in hand with high risk. In fact, he knows that the investment landscape is littered with the graves of small technology companies such as Data-Trix. For every Microsoft, dozens of other companies have failed. And one can rarely differentiate them in the early stages.*
>
> *By the rules of his profession, Jean-Michel should disclose the risks of the investments he advocates. But experience has taught him an important fact of investor behavior: Dwelling too much on the risks discourages clients from making a transaction. And if he fails to make the sale, neither he nor the brokerage firm will receive any commission income. So, he wonders, "How far should I go in discussing the risks with this client?"*

In this case, Jean-Michel's expertise and stock market experience have given him a measure of influence over his client. How should he use that influence? Clearly, if he speaks to the benefits of owning the newly issued shares, he is obliged to be equally forthcoming about the risks.

A Solution

Power, influence, and persuasion are necessary as well as dangerous, and they create ethical dilemmas. Some people must have greater power than others in order to influence behavior and make tough decisions. But that same power can be used in malicious ways. People must also apply persuasion in order to get things done; but powers of persuasion are always only a step away from self-serving manipulation.

Can anything be done to neutralize or eliminate the ethical dilemmas associated with power, influence, and persuasion? The answer is yes. Top management and corporate boards can reduce or eliminate them by doing the following:

- Aligning company policies and standards with the highest legal and ethical expectations of behavior.

- Zealously enforcing those policies and standards.

- Including ethical performance in appraisals of individual job performance—and taking them seriously.

- Seeing to it that executives and managers who are invested with power are morally and ethically equipped to use it wisely.

- Acting as visible models of ethical behavior by acting wisely and temperately in their use of power, influence, and persuasion. Senior managers can be models of ethical behavior only if they get out of their offices and interact with people at lower levels.

These five activities may seem like idealistic solutions, but they are easily within the capacity of senior managers and the directors to whom they ultimately report. Together, they can create a culture of ethical behavior that is self-policing and self-perpetuating and that sets a high standard for all employees.

Power, influence, and persuasion can be used for both good and evil. The challenge for management is to create an organizational culture in which the good side prevails.

Summing Up

- Power used ethically conforms to each of these standards: It is exercised to benefit the entity from which power is derived and that it is responsible to serve, and it conforms to cultural or legal standards of ethical behavior. The second of these standards trumps the first.

- Ethical influence and persuasion are most effective when based on mutual gain.

- Manipulation is the greatest ethical danger in the exercise of influence.

- Senior managers and directors can reduce or eliminate ethical problems if they (1) align company policies and standards with the highest legal and ethical expectations of behavior, (2) enforce those policies and standards, (3) include ethical performance in appraisals of job performance, (4) make certain that people given power have the moral and ethical capacity to use it wisely, and (5) act as models of ethical behavior.

Leading When You're Not the Boss

Many people find themselves in situations when they have management or leadership responsibility but no corresponding formal authority. Perhaps you head up a cross-functional team whose members don't report to you. Perhaps you manage a set of outside vendors. In these and similar cases, issuing direct orders is not feasible. Nevertheless, you must lead.

True leadership, of course, has never been a matter of formal authority. Leaders are effective when the people around them acknowledge them as leaders because of their personal qualities: their attributes, attitudes, and behaviors.

There is no single best way to lead when you are not the boss. Different situations—a crisis, a long-term project, and so forth—call for different types of leaders. Nevertheless, the following five-step approach can help you in many situations when you do not have a boss-subordinate relationship with others. It was developed by Harvard negotiation specialist Roger Fisher and his colleague Alan Sharp, who contend that it can be applied to virtually any project, team, or meeting in which you are a participant.

STEP 1: ESTABLISH GOALS. People accomplish the most when their objectives are clear. It follows that any group's first order of business should be to write down exactly what it hopes to achieve. The person who asks the question "Can we start by clarifying our goals?" and who then assumes the lead in discussing and drafting those goals is taking a leadership role, whatever his or her formal position.

STEP 2: THINK SYSTEMATICALLY. Observe your next meeting: People typically plunge into the issue at hand and start arguing over what to do. Effective leaders, in contrast, are more systematic—that is, they gather and lay out the pertinent data, seek out the causes of the situation, and propose actions based on their analysis. By engaging group members in this type of systematic approach and guiding them through it, they become de facto leaders. Their leadership keeps people focused on the problem-solving process, and they reinforce their leadership by asking appropriate questions.

"Do we have all the information we need to analyze this situation?"

"Can we focus on the causes of the problem we're trying to solve?"

Once they have determined the cause of the problem, they lead people in a similar systematic discussion of potential solutions.

STEP 3: LEARN FROM EXPERIENCE—WHILE IT'S HAPPENING. Most teams plow ahead on a project, and only when it's over do they conduct an after-action review to reflect on what they have learned. But sometimes it's more effective to learn as you go along, and this means that part of a group's daily work is to conduct mini-reviews and make any necessary midcourse corrections.

Why is this ongoing process more effective than an after-action review? The answer is that the data is fresh in everyone's mind. The reviews engage people's attention because the group can use its conclusions to make adjustments. Here, too, anyone who focuses the group on regular review and learning plays a de facto leadership role.

STEP 4: ENGAGE OTHERS. Successful groups engage the skills and efforts of every member. This doesn't happen naturally; someone must make it happen. A leader does this by seeking the best fit possible between members' interests and skills and the tasks that need doing. You can fill this role by writing a list of all the tasks that need doing and matching them with individuals or subgroups. If no one wants a particular task, brainstorm ways to make it more interesting or challenging. Partition the task if necessary into small parts that others can manage. Also, draw out the group's quieter members so that everyone feels like part of the team.

STEP 5: PROVIDE FEEDBACK. Even if you're not the boss, you can provide helpful feedback. Simply indicating your appreciation of the efforts of others will cost you nothing but will win people to your side: "I thought you did a great job in there."

Given the popularity of teams, managers at every level can find opportunities to act as leaders without formal authority. Use those opportunities whenever you confront a leadership vacuum or whenever stepping forward can improve the situation. The experience you develop through these situations will help you increase your personal power and improve your effectiveness as a manager and leader. And always remember, if you learn to lead successfully *without* formal authority, leading *with* it will be easy.

Useful Implementation Tools

This appendix contains tools that are useful when you assess an audience that you need to persuade and when you assess your own personal ability to persuade others. All the tools are adapted from Harvard ManageMentor®, an online product of Harvard Business School Publishing. Readers can freely access worksheets, checklists, and interactive tools on the *Harvard Business Essentials* Web site: www.elearning.hbsp.org/businesstools.

Understanding Your Audience

How can you assess and persuade your audience? The worksheet in figure B-1 can be used to clarify the main points of your proposal and assess the audience you are trying to influence and persuade.

Assessing Your Persuasion Skills

Use the tool in figure B-2 to assess your persuasion abilities.

FIGURE B-1

Worksheet for Audience Assessment

Use this tool to assess an audience that you will need to persuade.

Part I: Description of Your Proposal and Its Benefits

What is the idea or proposition that you plan to communicate to your audience?

What do you hope to persuade your audience to do based on that idea or proposition?

List the benefits of your idea or proposition.

Part II: Audience Assessment

1. *In the first column, list the names of the people whom you will need to persuade. These individuals will include the following:*
   - *Decision makers—individuals who approve or reject your idea*
   - *Stakeholders—people who are affected by acceptance of your proposal*
   - *Influencers—people who have access to the stakeholders and decision makers and can sway their opinions*
2. *In the second column, list the benefits that you think each audience member values most.*
3. *In the third column, note how you would gauge each audience member's receptivity to your idea. Which individuals are hostile, supportive, uninterested, uninformed, or neutral?*
4. *In the fourth column, list each audience member's preferred decision-making style. For example, which individuals want a lot of factual information before making a decision? Which ones prefer to analyze other respected individuals' decisions and follow their lead? Which ones tend to feel enthusiastic about new ideas early on but then look for data to support the proposed idea? Which ones, in general, are initially skeptical of others' ideas?*

Name	Benefits	Receptivity to Your Idea	Decision-Making Style
Decision Makers			
Stakeholders			
Influencers			

Part III: Action Planning

1. *In the first column, copy the names of the individuals just as you listed them in Part II.*

2. *In the second column, note how you plan to win each audience member's mind. That is, what benefits of your idea will you emphasize? What evidence will you provide to reassure your audience that those benefits are within their reach? What words will you use?*

3. *In the third column, note how you plan to win each audience member's heart. That is, what vivid descriptions, metaphors, analogies, and stories might you provide to connect with your listeners on an emotional level?*

4. *In the fourth column, note how you plan to acknowledge resisters' concerns and communicate your understanding of their concerns.*

Name	Actions to Win Minds	Actions to Win Hearts	Actions to Deal with Resistance
Decision Makers			
Stakeholders			
Influencers			

Part IV: Activating Triggers and Audience Self-Persuasion

What persuasion triggers might you set in motion before your presentation? For example, if you think the reciprocity trigger might increase your persuasiveness, what favors or kindnesses might you do for your audience members that would boost the likelihood that they'll support your idea in return?

How might you activate audience self-persuasion during your presentation? For example, what disturbing, leading, and rhetorical questions might you pose to encourage listeners to persuade *themselves* of the value of your idea?

Source: Harvard ManageMentor® on Persuasion, adapted with permission.

Worksheet for Persuasion Self-Assessment

Part I: Assessment

Use this tool to assess your persuasion abilities. For each statement below, indicate how accurately the statement describes you. "1" indicates "Not true," "5" indicates "Very true." Be sure to answer based on your actual *behavior in real workplace situations. In that way, you'll have the most accurate assessment of your skills.*

Statement	Rating Not true				Very true
1. I appropriately establish my qualifications before I try to persuade.	1	2	3	4	5
2. When persuading, I offer proof of how people have been able to trust me in the past.	1	2	3	4	5
3. I analyze listeners' words and behavior to assess their decision-making style and receptivity.	1	2	3	4	5
4. When persuading, I describe the benefits and unique aspects of my idea.	1	2	3	4	5
5. I use metaphors, analogies, and stories in my presentations to highlight my key points.	1	2	3	4	5
6. I consciously limit the number of points I make in my presentations to no more than three or four.	1	2	3	4	5
7. I support my arguments with highly credible evidence.	1	2	3	4	5
8. When I cite facts, data, or statistics, I package the information for clarity and memorability.	1	2	3	4	5
9. I encourage feedback from my listeners to activate audience self-persuasion.	1	2	3	4	5
10. I use disturbing, leading, and rhetorical questions to encourage audience self-persuasion.	1	2	3	4	5
11. I actively listen to my audience and reflect the content and emotions behind their statements.	1	2	3	4	5
12. I analyze my audience *before* persuading, to determine my strategy.	1	2	3	4	5
13. I tailor my persuasion strategy, material, and approach to different audiences.	1	2	3	4	5
14. I vary my choice of media according to the message I want to communicate.	1	2	3	4	5
15. I consciously help others in an effort to build trust and credibility, knowing that this may result in a relationship in which others want to help me later.	1	2	3	4	5
16. I try to encourage people to make their commitments to my ideas publicly or on paper.	1	2	3	4	5

Statement	Rating
	Not true *Very true*
17. I consciously tap the power that comes from titles or positions of authority that I hold.	1 2 3 4 5
18. When I possess exclusive information, I emphasize its scarcity value to those I'm persuading.	1 2 3 4 5
19. When I promote something, I stress that it's standard practice or part of a popular trend.	1 2 3 4 5
20. I associate myself with products, people, or companies that my audience admires.	1 2 3 4 5
21. I emphasize the similarities I share with people I want to persuade.	1 2 3 4 5
22. When I encounter resistance to my idea, I use paraphrasing and questioning to understand the source of the resistance and to communicate my understanding of the resisters' concerns.	1 2 3 4 5
23. I try to establish positive relationships and feelings with people I want to persuade.	1 2 3 4 5
24. When I anticipate encountering resistance to my ideas, I raise and understand opponents' arguments *before* presenting my own views.	1 2 3 4 5
25. I use affirmative, assertive speech and win-win language while persuading.	1 2 3 4 5
Score for each column	

Total score

(Calculate your score by adding up the numbers in all your responses.)

Part II: Scoring

Use the following table to interpret your score.

104–125	**Exceptional:** You're a talented persuader with a solid understanding of the art and science of persuasion.
78–103	**Superior:** You're a highly effective persuader in many areas but would benefit from refining some of your skills.
51–77	**Adequate:** You know and practice many of the basics of persuasion. However, you can increase your success by further extending your skills.
25–50	**Deficient:** You'll need to work broadly on your persuasion skills to begin changing or reinforcing others' attitudes, beliefs, and behaviors.

Source: Adapted from Harry Mills, *Artful Persuasion: How to Command Attention, Change Minds, and Influence People* (New York: AMACOM, 2000). Used with permission.

Commonsense Rules for Presentation Visuals

Formal presentations are an important tool of persuasion in modern organizations. Visual images containing text or graphics have become a standard feature in these presentations, so it is imperative that you master them.

Software programs such as Microsoft's PowerPoint, Corel Presentations, Harvard Graphics, and others have made it possible for businesspeople to enhance their presentations with eye-catching text, charts, and graphs. The programs offer numerous color and design features: three-dimensional effects, many font choices, clip art, and much more.

When used judiciously, these programs can create visuals that convey more information in less time than would more traditionally prepared visual aids. The high-tech visuals can get key points across and make them memorable. In the wrong hands, however, these powerful tools can actually confuse or bore the audience, diminishing the impact of an entire presentation. Here are a few rules for making the most of presentation visuals.

Rule 1: Subordinate Your Visuals to Your Message

You and what you have to say should always be the focus of the presentation. Visuals should therefore play no more than a supportive role. They should never command center stage. Presenters can observe this important rule by following these guidelines:

- Don't try to say everything through overheads.
- Refrain from simply reading your overheads to the audience.
- Avoid visuals that are not essential to the presentation.

Rule 2: Keep Your Visuals Simple

Some presenters clutter every overhead with border-to-border text, as in example A. Extra words detract from the presenter's message

---

Example A [Cluttered]: Challenges for the Coming Year

The sales force must become more efficient next year. Currently, selling costs are running close to 20 percent of revenues. The industry average is 14 percent.

On average, we have fifteen days of finished goods inventory. Financing and maintaining that inventory are expensive. If we were better at forecasting sales, we could cut that inventory level—perhaps by as much as four days. That would save the company close to $50,000 per year.

Our work force needs more training to stay competitive. We should aim for forty hours of training for all nonprofessional employees and sixty hours for professional employees.

Example B [Simple]: Challenges for the Coming Year

- Greater sales efficiency
- Less finished goods inventory
- More training for everyone

and make the audience work unnecessarily hard to capture key points.

Example A is overburdened with text. It contains information that would be better conveyed verbally by the speaker. Example B, in contrast, captures the key points without the supporting details. These points are clear and easy to remember.

Rule 3: Use a Minimum of Devices

People who take the time to master presentation software are tempted to use many of their "cool" devices: different colors, many font styles and sizes, shading, and on and on. Don't fall into this trap. Those devices can deflect attention from the message. Ask yourself, "Do I need the fancy fill effects and the clip art? Would one font style be better than the three I'm using?" In most cases, your visuals will look more professional if you use a bare minimum of devices. Simpler is usually better.

Rule 4: Make Your Images Large and Legible

Your visuals should be clearly legible to everyone in the room—even those in the back row of seats. If you've observed rules 2 and 3, then you'll have plenty of room on each slide or overhead to make your images large.

Rule 5: Use Graphics to Tell Key Parts of the Story

Most people are visually oriented. They perceive and digest information best when it's presented graphically.

For example, suppose a speaker wants to make the point that one product model has outsold two others. He could simply tell his audience, "Results for the previous twelve months indicate that model C outsold both models A and B." He could also put this information in an overhead sheet containing the following sentence: "Model C has outsold both model A and model B during the past twelve months." The speaker could then go on to detail the relative sales of these three models.

Alternatively, he could use a graphic image that shows the relative sales performance of the three models in unit numbers (figure C-1).

To create the greatest impact, reserve graphics like those in figure C-1 for the key points of your presentation. If you create visuals for everything, the key points will be lost in the clutter.

Rule 6: Use the Most Appropriate Graphic Form

Most presentation programs and their spreadsheet supporting systems allow you to produce pie charts, column charts, bar charts, line charts, column charts, scattergrams, and so forth. Each is best for presenting certain types of data.

FIGURE C-1

Presenting Sales Figures Graphically

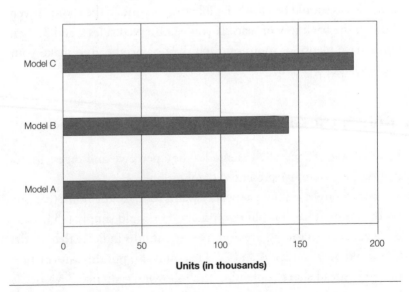

Pie Charts

Pie charts are best when your goal is to show the impact of different factors on the whole. Thus, if you wanted your audience to understand the contributions of your company's three product models to total sales revenue, a pie chart would be your best choice (see figure C-2). Each is shown as a slice of the entire pie.

Bar and Column Charts

Use bar and column charts when you want the audience to compare outcomes, such as in the model A, B, C bar chart shown earlier in figure C-1. In that chart, the audience can see *both* the relative performances of the three models and their actual unit sales. That's something they won't see in a pie chart.

Line Charts

Line charts are particularly good for indicating trends. In figure C-3, we show the change in the share price of XYZ Corporation over

FIGURE C-2

Using a Pie Chart to Show the Effect of Parts on the Whole

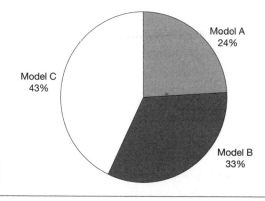

Appendix C

FIGURE C-3

Using a Line Chart to Show Change over Time

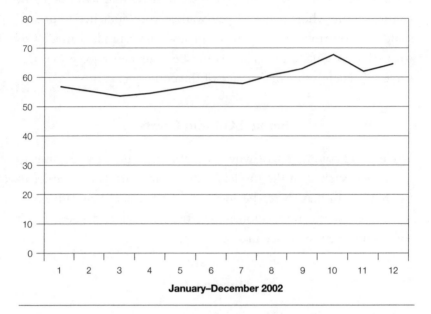

January–December 2002

time—January through December 2002. If we were comparing its price trend to that of a competitor, we could easily put them on the same chart.

Scattergrams

If you want to show a statistical linear regression (the best fit of a line drawn through a number of scattered data points), exponential smoothing, or a moving average, a scattergram is your best bet. These charts are invaluable when you have many data points for one specific variable—for example, the merchandise returns from fifty branch stores for each month of a year. Figure C-4 maps data points along the x- (time) and y- (returns) axes. In the figure, we created a best-fit trend line based on statistical linear regression for a vendor's merchandise returns over eighteen months. The audience can see at

FIGURE C-4

Scattergram with Linear Trend Line

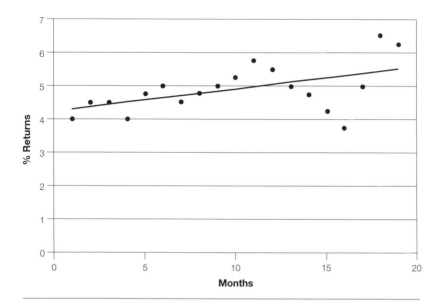

a glance the direction that returns are taking, even though the monthly percentage returns are scattered around.

Rule 7: Label the Key Features of Your Graphics

Make sure that your audience will understand at a glance what the quantitative data in your graphics represent. For example, the top graph in figure C-5 shows data for a particular company. But what does each column represent? Complaints per salesperson? Total sales revenues? District sales revenues? A month or a quarter of revenues? Are the values on the vertical axis dollars or thousands of dollars? Or are they euros?

In the labeled version of the same chart in figure C-5, the audience can now see that each column represents the dollar value of

FIGURE C-5

Labels Help Clarify Data

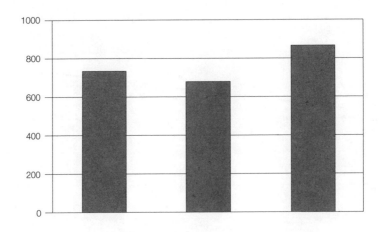

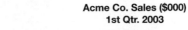

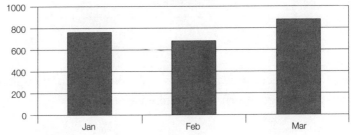

Acme Company sales, expressed in thousands, for the first three months of 2003.

With the availability of graphics software, it has become easier than ever to prepare illustrations for your presentations. If you observe these seven rules for the use of graphics, your presentations will be more professional and more effective.

Notes

Introduction

1. John P. Kotter, "Power, Dependence, and Effective Management," *Harvard Business Review*, July–August 1977, 125–126.

Chapter 1

1. Rosabeth Moss Kanter, "Power Failure in Management Circuits," *Harvard Business Review*, July–August 1979, 65.

2. Ibid.

3. Jeffrey Pfeffer, *Managing With Power* (Boston: Harvard Business School Press, 1992), 9.

4. David C. McClelland and David H. Burnham, "Power Is the Great Motivator," *Harvard Business Review*, January 2003, 117–126.

5. Ibid.

Chapter 2

1. John P. Kotter, "Power, Dependence, and Effective Management," *Harvard Business Review*, July–August 1977, 128.

2. For an expanded treatment of Deming's role in reshaping postwar Japan, see Richard Luecke, *Scuttle Your Ships Before Advancing* (New York: Oxford University Press, 1994), 64–76.

3. Jeffrey Pfeffer, *Managing With Power* (Boston: Harvard Business School Press, 1992), 63–64.

Chapter 3

1. B. Kim Barnes, *Exercising Influence* (Berkeley, CA: Barnes & Conti Associates, 2000), 9.

2. For the details of this story, see Gregory H. Watson, *Strategic Benchmarking* (New York: John Wiley & Sons, 1993), 129–148.

3. Allan R. Cohen and David L. Bradford, *Influence Without Authority* (New York: John Wiley & Sons, 1989), 73.

Chapter 4

1. Jeffrey Pfeffer, *Managing With Power* (Boston: Harvard Business School Press, 1992), 203.

2. Thomas Johnson and Robert Kaplan, *Relevance Lost: The Decline and Fall of Management Accounting* (Boston: Harvard Business School Press, 1987).

Chapter 5

1. This chapter draws heavily on material found in the Persuasion module of Harvard ManageMentor®, an online product of Harvard Business School Publishing.

2. These questions were contributed by Professor Kathleen Reardon. They are from the inventory of persuasive skills found in her forthcoming book, *It's All Politics* (New York: Currency/Doubleday, 2005).

3. Michael D. Watkins, "The Power to Persuade," Note 9-800-323, Harvard Business School Publishing, revised July 24, 2000.

Chapter 6

1. This chapter draws heavily on material found in the Persuasion module of Harvard ManageMentor®, an online product of Harvard Business School Publishing.

2. Persuasion triggers were first developed and explained by Robert B. Cialdini in his article, "Harnessing the Science of Persuasion," *Harvard Business Review,* OnPoint Enhanced Edition, October 2001.

Chapter 7

1. The discussion of the Greek method of presentation is adapted from "Presentations and the Ancient Greeks," *Harvard Management Communication Letter,* January 1999, 5–8.

2. This section on the styles of learning is adapted from "Presentations That Appeal to All of Your Listeners," *Harvard Management Communication Letter,* June 2000, 4–5.

3. This section is adapted from Constantine Von Hoffman, Richard Bierck, Michael Hattersley, and Nick Wreden, "Handling Q&A: The Five Kinds of Listening," *Harvard Management Update,* February 1999.

Chapter 8

1. Philip G. Zimbardo, *The Boston Globe,* May 9, 2004. View at <www.boston.com/news/globe/editorial_opinion/oped/articles/2004/05/09/power_turns_good_soldiers_into_bad_apples>.

2. As told in Richard Leifer, Christopher McDermott, Gina Colarelli O'Connor, Lois Peters, Mark Rice, and Robert Veryzer, *Radical Innovation* (Boston: Harvard Business School Press, 2000), 56–57.

3. Joseph L. Badaracco Jr. and Allen P. Weber, "Business Ethics: A View from the Trenches," *California Management Review*, Vol. 37, no. 2 (Winter 1995) 8–9.

4. Allan R. Cohen and David L. Bradford, *Influence Without Authority* (New York: John Wiley & Sons, 1991), ix.

5. Ibid., x.

Glossary

AFFILIATIVE MANAGER Per David McClelland and David Burnham, a manager who is more interested in being liked than in having and using power to get the job done.

ANTITHESIS A rhetorical device that places a sentence or one of its parts in opposition to another in order to capture attention or to evoke a strong response.

CENTER OF INFLUENCE An individual having the power to influence those around him or her.

COALITION A temporary alliance of separate entities or individuals who join together to seek a common purpose. See also *natural coalition and single-issue coalition*.

CURRENCIES OF EXCHANGE Per Allan Cohen and David Bradford, the coinage of influence; resources that can be offered to a potential ally in exchange for cooperation.

EMPATHY The ability to identify with or vicariously experience the thoughts or feelings of others.

INFLUENCE The mechanism through which people use power to change behavior or attitudes. Unlike power, influence can produce an effect without the apparent exertion of force, compulsion, or direct command.

INFLUENCE NETWORK A network of individuals through which influence is made or enforced. In this network, some individuals have greater influence than others.

INFLUENCERS Individuals who participate indirectly in the decision-making process. They provide advice and information to key stakeholders and decision makers.

INSTITUTIONAL MANAGER   Per David McClelland and David Burnham, a manager who deploys power in the service of the organization and not in service of personal goals.

LAW OF RECIPROCITY   A general rule that demands that every favor must someday be repaid.

MANIPULATION   Per Allan Cohen and David Bradford, actions taken to achieve influence that would be rendered less effective if the other party knew the manipulator's actual intentions.

METAPHOR   An imaginative way of describing something as something else—for example, "Business is war." When a metaphor shapes some-one's viewpoint, it becomes an *organizing metaphor*.

NATURAL COALITION   A coalition of allies who share a broad range of common interests.

OPINION LEADER   See *center of influence*.

ORGANIZING METAPHOR   An overarching worldview that shapes a per-son's everyday actions—for example, "Business is war." See also *metaphor*.

PARALLEL STRUCTURE   A rhetorical device that uses sentence elements that are alike in both function and construction—for example, "We will work hard. We will work smart. We will not tire or fail."

PERSONAL POWER   Power that is a function of one or many qualities: ideas, expertise, accomplishments, charisma, communication skill, and trustworthiness.

PERSONAL POWER MANAGER   Per scholars David McClelland and David Burnham, a manager whose personal need for power exceeds his need to be liked. This manager seeks power for himself and for people on his team in order to get the job done. Subordinates like this kind of boss and often become very loyal because the boss makes them feel strong. On the negative side, this manager is a power aggrandizer and turf builder and not a good institution builder.

PERSUASION   A process through which one can change or reinforce the attitudes, opinions, or behaviors of others.

POWER   The potential to allocate resources and to make and enforce decisions.

POWER OF POSITION The power or authority associated with one's formal position in an organization.

RELATIONAL POWER Informal power that emerges from one's relationships with others.

RHETORICAL QUESTION A question asked for the sole purpose of producing an effect on the audience. The speaker does not expect the question to be answered—least of all by the audience.

SINGLE-ISSUE COALITION A coalition of parties that differ on other issues but unite to support or block a single issue (often for different reasons).

TRIAD A rhetorical device that uses a list of three items.

For Further Reading

Books

Barnes, B. Kim. *Exercising Influence: A Guide for Making Things Happen at Work, at Home, and in Your Community*. Berkeley, CA: Barnes & Conti, 2000. The author draws on her experience as an organizational consultant to explain how you can employ influence to accomplish more in the three major arenas of life: work, home, and community. One interesting feature is the author's chapter on influence planning.

Cohen, Allan R., and David L. Bradford. *Influence Without Authority*. New York: John Wiley & Sons, 1989. Written by two outstanding business scholars, this book addresses a problem faced by a growing number of managers: how to lead when they are thrust into positions of responsibility with no corresponding authority. The authors describe how to obtain the cooperation of managers who control resources and information but who are not obliged to cooperate. Points in the book are nicely illustrated with case examples.

Kotter, John P. *Power and Influence*. New York: Free Press, 1985. In the complex world of work, things no longer get done simply because someone issues an order and someone else follows it. Most of us work in socially intricate organizations where we need the help not only of subordinates but also of colleagues, superiors, and outsiders to accomplish our goals. This often leaves us facing a "power gap" because we must depend on people over whom we have little or no explicit control. This book is about how to bridge that gap: how to exercise power and influence to get things done through others when your responsibilities exceed your formal authority. Kotter explains how to develop sufficient resources of unofficial power and influence to achieve goals, steer clear of conflicts, foster creative team behavior, and gain the cooperation and support you need from subordinates, coworkers, superiors—even people outside your department or organization. He also shows how you can avoid the twin traps of naivete and cynicism when dealing with power relationships, and how to use power without abusing it.

Ludwig, Arnold D. *King of the Mountain: The Nature of Political Leadership.* Louisville: University of Kentucky Press, 2002. In this book, emeritus professor of psychiatry Arnold Ludwig reports the results of his study of 377 world leaders and his thoughts about why people seek to rule (i.e., why they seek power). One of his observations is that power seekers are very similar to alpha male primates, who are driven to establish themselves as the dominant members of their groups. Readers will enjoy the author's analysis of Idi Amin, Tony Blair, Winston Churchill, Ronald Reagan, and others, and the factors that drove them to seek power.

Mills, Harry. *Artful Persuasion: How to Command Attention, Change Minds, and Influence People.* New York: AMACOM, 2000. Mills makes it clear that anyone can learn to be a skilled persuader. In this book, he explores the psychology behind persuasion and reveals how the most successful persuaders work their magic. Exploring both the conscious and unconscious forces at play, Mills provides practical guidelines for tackling the toughest challenges of persuasion—such as winning over hostile audiences, connecting emotionally with audiences, and getting your audiences to persuade themselves to support your ideas.

Pfeffer, Jeffrey. *Managing With Power: Politics and Influence in Organizations.* Boston: Harvard Business School Press, 1992. Stanford management scholar Pfeffer looks at the role of power and influence in organizations, revealing how individuals gain it and use to get things done. He argues that anyone can cultivate an awareness of how power works and increase one's own influence. Examples are drawn from business, politics, science, and even religious cults.

Reardon, Kathleen. *The Secret Handshake: Mastering The Politics of The Business Inner Circle.* New York: Doubleday, 2000. This book covers an aspect of power not found in our Essentials on the subject. In The Secret Handshake, Kathleen Reardon reveals the unwritten rule of organizational politics that govern so much of business life. Her many candid interviews with corporate executives provide a window into the netherworld of organizational life, and offers practical advice for being noticed, networking, accomplishing your goals, and knowing when to persuade and when to fight. Professor Reardon's second book on this subject, It's All Politics, will be made available through the same publisher in 2005. Like the first, it addresses the important role that politics plays in facilitating or hindering power, influence, and persuasion.

Notes and Articles

Cialdini, Robert B. "Harnessing the Science of Persuasion." *Harvard Business Review*, OnPoint Enhanced Edition, October 2001. Cialdini shines the spotlight on persuasion triggers—the subconscious mental shortcuts people take to make decisions when they're pressed for time, fatigued, or distracted. Drawing from the behavioral sciences, Cialdini explores the following triggers: liking (people like those who like them), reciprocity (people repay favors in kind), social proof (people follow the lead of others like themselves), consistency (people align with clear commitments), authority (people defer to experts), and scarcity (people want more of what they have less of).

Conger, Jay A. "The Necessary Art of Persuasion." *Harvard Business Review*, OnPoint Enhanced Edition, May–June 1998. This article defines and explains the four essential elements of persuasion. Business today is run largely by teams and populated by authority-averse baby boomers and generation Xers. That makes persuasion more important than ever as a managerial tool. But contrary to popular belief, asserts author Jay Conger (director of the Leadership Institute of the University of Southern California's Marshall Business School), persuasion is not the same as selling an idea or convincing opponents to see things your way. Instead, it is a process of learning from others and negotiating a shared solution. To that end, persuasion consists of these essential elements: establishing credibility, framing to find common ground, providing vivid evidence, and connecting emotionally. Persuasion can be a force for enormous good in an organization, but people must understand it for what it is: an often painstaking process that requires insight, planning, and compromise.

Hattersley, Michael. "Persuasion." Note 9-392-012. Boston: Harvard Business School Publishing, September 19, 1991. This note examines the principles that apply in any persuasive business situation. It describes how to analyze the goals and audience; how to devise a persuasive message; and how to execute a persuasive strategy in writing, presentations, and larger corporate communication tasks.

Long-Lingo, Elizabeth, and Kathleen McGinn. "Power and Influence: Achieving Your Objectives in Organizations." Note 9-801-425. Boston: Harvard Business School Publishing, April 4, 2002. Power, as described in this HBS class note, is the potential to mobilize energy. This rather neutral definition does not address the issues of how to exercise power or to what ends. The answers to these questions determine the ultimate

value of an individual's power. This note is written to help you analyze
the social system in which your power exists and your influence will be
used. Following the guidelines presented, a careful analysis of the social
system in which an individual operates and an assessment of that individual's desires and objectives within the social system may help maximize
the development of power and the effective use of influence.

Marton, Betty A. "Mastering the Art of Persuasion." *Harvard Management
Communication Letter*, July 2000. Marton surveys the experts' thinking
on the subject of persuasion, listing do's and don'ts for aspiring as well as
seasoned persuaders—for example, do develop empathy so that you can
accurately perceive how others feel, and do become an effective team
builder. You'll learn how to build a coalition of support so that you
know whom to go to when you need to make a pitch. But don't take a
strong position at the start of your persuasion effort; you'll only give potential resisters something to fight against. And don't confuse argument
with persuasion. Arguing your position is only one part of effective persuasion. You'll also need to rely on effective communication, empathy,
and emotional connection with your audiences.

McClelland, David C., and David H. Burnham. "Power Is the Great Motivator." *Harvard Business Review*, January 2003. To motivate others,
managers must be motivated themselves. The key issue here is the
source of the motivation—the way the manager defines success. Some
equate success with personal achievement; others see success as being
liked by others. To succeed in a complex organization, a manager needs
to have a power motivation, which is not a dictatorial impulse but rather
the desire to have an impact, to be strong and influential. This power,
according to the authors, must be disciplined and channeled in ways that
benefit the organization and not the manager herself.

Simpson, Liz. "Get Around Resistance and Win Over the Other Side."
Harvard Management Communication Letter, April 2003. Simpson focuses
on the crucial obstacle that most persuaders encounter numerous times:
opposition to their ideas. She explains how to "step into your opponent's shoes" by discerning the concerns and emotions fueling the resistance. By listening closely, you demonstrate that you're taking the
resister's interests to heart and earning his trust. He then becomes more
open to seeing things from your perspective. In addition to listening,
make your verbal and nonverbal messages consistent and present your
resister's point of view before your own.

Watkins, Michael D. "The Power to Persuade." Note 9-800-323. Boston:
Harvard Business School Publishing, July 2000. Revised July 24, 2000.
Watkins explains how to master core persuasion tasks. For example, to

map the influence landscape, identify whom you need to persuade; decide who your supporters, opponents, and "persuadables" are; assess their interests and the reasons for any resistance; and figure out what they see as their alternatives to the change you're proposing. To shape perceptions of interests, introduce rewards for desired behavior and impose disincentives for undesired behavior. Also frame your pitch deliberately—for example, by heightening concerns about loss or risk or linking the proposed change to your audience's core values. To gain acceptance for tough decisions, create a fair process by which your audience feels you've taken their concerns and ideas into account.

Williams, Gary A., and Robert B. Miller. "Change the Way You Persuade." *Harvard Business Review*, OnPoint Enhanced Edition, May 2002. The authors urge persuaders to tailor their efforts to their audience members' decision-making styles. Different individuals, they maintain, have different preferences for deciding whether to accept an idea. Each wants certain kinds of information at specific steps in the decision-making process. There are five styles that most persuaders will likely encounter in the workplace:

Charismatic: easily enthralled but bases final decisions on balanced information

Thinker: needs extensive detail

Skeptic: challenges every data point

Follower: relies on her own or others' past decisions

Controller: Implements only his own ideas

For each style, the authors lay out corresponding strategies and examples of how to implement them.

Index

About the Subject Adviser

KATHLEEN K. REARDON, Ph.D., Professor of Management and Organization in the University of Southern California Marshall School of Business, is a leading authority on persuasion, negotiation, and politics in the workplace. She is the author of seven books and numerous articles published in leading communication and business journals, including the *Harvard Business Review*. Her book *The Secret Handshake: Mastering the Politics of the Business Inner Circle*, released in early 2001 (Doubleday), rapidly became a business bestseller in the United States. Dr. Reardon's most recent books include *The Skilled Negotiator* (Jossey-Bass), *On Becoming a Skilled Negotiator* (Wiley), and *It's All Politics* (Currency/Doubleday).

Dr. Reardon has served on the prestigious *Harvard Business Review* McKinsey Award Panel and the editorial boards of several academic journals. She was elected to the board of the International Communication Association and the founding advisory board of First Star, an organization devoted to promoting the rights of children. In 2004 she was designated the first Distinguished Research Scholar of The Irish Management Institute.

Dr. Reardon is a Phi Beta Kappa graduate of the University of Connecticut (B.A.) and received her M.A. and Ph.D. summa cum laude and with distinction from the University of Massachusetts at Amherst.

About the Writer

RICHARD LUECKE is the writer of several books in the *Harvard Business Essentials* series. Based in Salem, Massachusetts, Mr. Luecke has authored or developed more than thirty books and dozens of articles on a wide range of business subjects. He has an M.B.A. from the University of St. Thomas. He can be reached at richard.luecke@verizon.net.

Harvard Business Review Paperback Series

The Harvard Business Review Paperback Series offers the best thinking on cutting-edge management ideas from the world's leading thinkers, researchers, and managers. Designed for leaders who believe in the power of ideas to change business, these books will be useful to managers at all levels of experience, but especially senior executives and general managers. In addition, this series is widely used in training and executive development programs.

Books are priced at $19.95 U.S.
Price subject to change.

Title	Product #
Harvard Business Review **Interviews with CEOs**	3294
Harvard Business Review on **Advances in Strategy**	8032
Harvard Business Review on **Becoming a High Performance Manager**	1296
Harvard Business Review on **Brand Management**	1445
Harvard Business Review on **Breakthrough Leadership**	8059
Harvard Business Review on **Breakthrough Thinking**	181X
Harvard Business Review on **Building Personal and Organizational Resilience**	2721
Harvard Business Review on **Business and the Environment**	2336
Harvard Business Review on **Change**	8842
Harvard Business Review on **Compensation**	701X
Harvard Business Review on **Corporate Ethics**	273X
Harvard Business Review on **Corporate Governance**	2379
Harvard Business Review on **Corporate Responsibility**	2748
Harvard Business Review on **Corporate Strategy**	1429
Harvard Business Review on **Crisis Management**	2352
Harvard Business Review on **Culture and Change**	8369
Harvard Business Review on **Customer Relationship Management**	6994
Harvard Business Review on **Decision Making**	5572
Harvard Business Review on **Effective Communication**	1437

To order, call 1-800-668-6780, or go online at www.HBSPress.org

Title	Product #
Harvard Business Review on **Entrepreneurship**	9105
Harvard Business Review on **Finding and Keeping the Best People**	5564
Harvard Business Review on **Innovation**	6145
Harvard Business Review on **Knowledge Management**	8818
Harvard Business Review on **Leadership**	8834
Harvard Business Review on **Leadership at the Top**	2756
Harvard Business Review on **Leading in Turbulent Times**	1806
Harvard Business Review on **Managing Diversity**	7001
Harvard Business Review on **Managing High-Tech Industries**	1828
Harvard Business Review on **Managing People**	9075
Harvard Business Review on **Managing the Value Chain**	2344
Harvard Business Review on **Managing Uncertainty**	9083
Harvard Business Review on **Managing Your Career**	1318
Harvard Business Review on **Marketing**	8040
Harvard Business Review on **Measuring Corporate Performance**	8826
Harvard Business Review on **Mergers and Acquisitions**	5556
Harvard Business Review on **Motivating People**	1326
Harvard Business Review on **Negotiation**	2360
Harvard Business Review on **Nonprofits**	9091
Harvard Business Review on **Organizational Learning**	6153
Harvard Business Review on **Strategic Alliances**	1334
Harvard Business Review on **Strategies for Growth**	8850
Harvard Business Review on **The Business Value of IT**	9121
Harvard Business Review on **The Innovative Enterprise**	130X
Harvard Business Review on **Turnarounds**	6366
Harvard Business Review on **What Makes a Leader**	6374
Harvard Business Review on **Work and Life Balance**	3286

To order, call 1-800-668-6780, or go online at www.HBSPress.org

Harvard Business Essentials

In the fast-paced world of business today, everyone needs a personal re-source—a place to go for advice, coaching, background information, or an-swers. The Harvard Business Essentials series fits the bill. Concise and straightforward, these books provide highly practical advice for readers at all levels of experience. Whether you are a new manager interested in ex-panding your skills or an experienced executive looking to stay on top, these solution-oriented books give you the reliable tips and tools you need to im-prove your performance and get the job done. Harvard Business Essentials titles will quickly become your constant companions and trusted guides.

These books are priced at $19.95 U.S., except as noted.
Price subject to change.

Title	Product #
Harvard Business Essentials: **Negotiation**	1113
Harvard Business Essentials: **Managing Creativity and Innovation**	1121
Harvard Business Essentials: **Managing Change and Transition**	8741
Harvard Business Essentials: **Hiring and Keeping the Best People**	875X
Harvard Business Essentials: **Finance for Managers**	8768
Harvard Business Essentials: **Business Communication**	113X
Harvard Business Essentials: **Manager's Toolkit ($24.95)**	2896
Harvard Business Essentials: **Managing Projects Large and Small**	3213
Harvard Business Essentials: **Creating Teams with an Edge**	290X
Harvard Business Essentials: **Entrepreneur's Toolkit**	4368
Harvard Business Essentials: **Coaching and Mentoring**	435X
Harvard Business Essentials: **Crisis Management**	4376
Harvard Business Essentials: **Time Management**	6336
Harvard Business Essentials: **Power, Influence, and Persuasion**	631X

To order, call 1-800-668-6780, or go online at www.HBSPress.org

The Results-Driven Manager

The Results-Driven Manager series collects timely articles from Harvard Management Update and Harvard Management Communication Letter to help senior to middle managers sharpen their skills, increase their effectiveness, and gain a competitive edge. Presented in a concise, accessible format to save managers valuable time, these books offer authoritative insights and techniques for improving job performance and achieving immediate results.

These books are priced at $14.95 U.S.
Price subject to change.

Title	Product #
The Results-Driven Manager:	
Face-to-Face Communications for Clarity and Impact	3477
The Results-Driven Manager:	
Managing Yourself for the Career You Want	3469
The Results-Driven Manager:	
Presentations That Persuade and Motivate	3493
The Results-Driven Manager: **Teams That Click**	3507
The Results-Driven Manager:	
Winning Negotiations That Preserve Relationships	3485
The Results-Driven Manager: **Dealing with Difficult People**	6344
The Results-Driven Manager: **Taking Control of Your Time**	6352
The Results-Driven Manager: **Getting People on Board**	6360